Christian Book of Records

Christian
Book of
Records

HENDRICKSON
PUBLISHERS

CONTENTS

114690

Part I

THE
BIBLE

1.1 STATISTICS

The Bible was written by human authors, each of whom was inspired by God. Little did the writers of the Bible imagine that their writings would be collected into one volume. This section concentrates on some of the amazing facts and figures which are often overlooked or unknown in this unique book.

WRITING THE BIBLE

✣ MOST DIVINELY INSPIRED WRITERS

The Bible was written over a 1,500-1,600 year period (1500 BC-AD 100) in three languages (Hebrew, Aramaic and Greek) by about 40 authors living in 10 different countries. 2,930 different people are depicted in the Bible in 1,551 places.

LOST BOOKS OF THE BIBLE

✣ UNKNOWN BOOKS

Enigmatic references to unknown books are scattered throughout the Bible. The *Book of Jashar* and the *Book of the Wars of Yahweh* are mentioned. These books cannot be read as no copies are known to exist.

Lost books cited in the Bible
- *The Book of the Wars of the Lord*, Numbers 21:14.
- *The Book of Jashar*, Joshua 10:12-13; 2 Samuel 1:19-27
- *The Chronicles of the kings of Judah*, mentioned 15 times
- *The Chronicles of the kings of Israel*, mentioned 18 times
- *The book of the annals of Solomon*, 1 Kings 11:41
- *Book of the kings of Israel*, 1 Chronicles 9:1; 2 Chronicles 20:34
- *Book of the kings of Judah and Israel*, 2 Chronicles 16:11
- *The annals of the kings of Israel*, 2 Chronicles 33:18
- *The records of Samuel the seer*, 1 Chronicles 29:29
- *The records of Gad the seer*, 1 Chronicles 29:29
- *The records of Nathan the prophet*, 1 Chronicles 29:29; 2 Chronicles 9:29
- *The prophecy of Ahijah the Shilonite*,

"Just about halfway then?"

2 Chronicles 9:29
- *The visions of Iddo the seer,*
  2 Chronicles 9:29
- *The records of Shemaiah the prophet and Iddo the seer,* 2 Chronicles 12:15
- *The annals of Jehu son of Hanani,*
  2 Chronicles 20:34
- *The records of the seers,*
  2 Chronicles 33:19
- *The annotations of the prophet Iddo,*
  2 Chronicles 13:22
- *The annotations on the book of the kings,*
  2 Chronicles 24:27

GOD IN THE BIBLE

✣ GOD IN BIBLE BOOKS
The proper name 'God' occurs 4,379 times and 'Lord' occurs 7,738 times.

✣ BOOK WITH NO MENTION OF GOD
The name 'God' does not appear in the book of Esther.

CHAPTERS, VERSES, WORDS AND LETTERS

✣ NUMBER OF CHAPTERS
There are 1,189 chapters in the Bible – 929 chapters in the Old Testament and 260 chapters in the New Testament.

✣ NUMBER OF VERSES
There are 31,173 verses in the Bible – 23,214 in the Old Testament and 7,959 in the New Testament.

✣ NUMBER OF WORDS
There are 592,493 words in the *KJV* Old Testament. There are 181,253 words in the *KJV* New Testament.

✣ NUMBER OF LETTERS
There are 2,728,100 letters in the *KJV* Old Testament and 838,380 letters in the *KJV* New Testament.

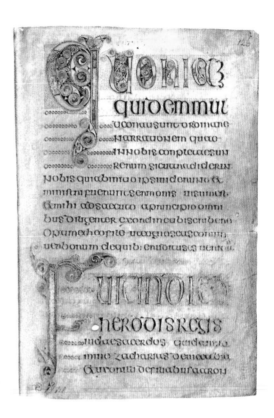

✣ LONGEST CHAPTER IN THE BIBLE
Psalm 119 is the longest chapter in the Bible with 176 verses. It is written as an alphabetic acrostic. The 176 verses are split up into 22 sections, each section starting with a successive letter of the Hebrew alphabet, which has 22 letters. Each of the eight verses in the 22 sections starts with same letter of the Hebrew alphabet.

✣ MIDDLE VERSE OF THE BIBLE
Psalm 118:8 is the middle verse of the Bible: 'It is better to take refuge in the LORD than to trust in man.'

✣ SHORTEST OLD TESTAMENT VERSE
The shortest verse in the Old Testament is 1 Chronicles 1:25: 'Eber, Peleg, Reu.'

✣ LONGEST VERSE
The longest verse is Esther 8:9: 'At once the royal secretaries were summoned – on the twenty-third day of the third month, the

A page from a 7th century illuminated manuscript from Ireland – the *Book of Durrow.*

month of Sivan. They wrote out all Mordecai's orders to the Jews, and to the satraps, governors and nobles of the 127 provinces stretching from India to Cush. These orders were written in the script of each province and the language of each people and also to the Jews in their own script and language.'

✠ SHORTEST VERSE IN THE ENGLISH BIBLE
The shortest verse in the English *King James Version* is John 11:35. It has just two words: 'Jesus wept.'

✠ THE SHORTEST VERSE IN THE GREEK BIBLE
The shortest verse in the Greek Bible is 1 Thessalonians 5:16. The Greek words are 'παντοτε χαιρετε', 'Be joyful always.' In the Greek this amounts to 14 letters, whereas John 11:35 ('Jesus wept.') has 16 letters in the Greek, 'εδακρυσεν ὁ Ιησους'.

✠ ONLY VERSE TO START AND END WITH 'ALL'
The only verse in the Bible, using the *King James Version*, that begins and ends with the word 'all' is Isaiah 53.6: 'All we like sheep have gone astray; we have turned every one to his own way; and the Lord hath laid on him the iniquity of us all.'

✠ FIRST BIBLES WITH CHAPTER AND VERSE DIVISIONS
Chapter and verse divisions are not part of the original Bible manuscripts. Three different people are credited with adding chapter divisions to the Latin *Vulgate:* the Archbishop of Canterbury, Lanfranc (d.1089), another Archbishop of Canterbury, Stephen Langton (d.1228), and Hugo de Sancto Caro of the 13th century. Verse numbers to the Greek New Testament were added in 1551 by the Parisian printer Robert Etienne.

READING THE BIBLE

✠ MEMORIZING OF THE BIBLE
Thomas Cranmer (1489-1556), Archbishop of Canterbury, reportedly memorized the whole Bible in only three months.

BOOKS OF THE BIBLE

✠ NUMBER OF BOOKS
There are 66 books in the Bible – or 39 books in the Old Testament and 27 books in the New Testament.

✠ CATHOLIC BIBLE, PROTESTANT BIBLE
The Catholic Bible has 73 books while the Protestant Bible has 66 books. This is because the Catholic Old Testament includes the seven books of the deutero-canonicals (or the apocryphal books) which were written in Greek.

✠ SHORTEST BOOK
Four New Testament books have a single chapter: 2 John, 3 John, Philemon and Jude. Philemon and Jude both have 25 verses. 2 John has 13 verses, with 303 words. 3 John has 14 verses, but fewest words, 299.

✠ LONGEST NEW TESTAMENT BOOK
The Acts of the Apostles is the longest New Testament book, with its 28 chapters, 1,007 verses, and 24,250 words.

Thomas Cranmer, Archbishop of Canterbury (1489–1556).

✣ **WHOLE BIBLE**

If the Bible were read aloud, as in a church service, it would take about 70 hours and 40 minutes to read the whole Bible, with the Old Testament taking about 52 hours and 20 minutes and the New Testament taking about 18 hours and 20 minutes.

BIBLE PEOPLE AND PLACES

✣ **OLDEST PERSON**

Methuselah, who lived 969 years (Genesis 5:27).

✣ **SECOND OLDEST PERSON**

Jared, who lived 962 years (Genesis 5:20).

✣ **LONGEST NAME OF PERSON**

The longest name in the Bible was given to one of Isaiah's sons, Maher-Shalal-Hash-Baz (Isaiah 8:1).

✣ **LONGEST NAME FOR A PLACE**

Four places, each with 16 letters, are mentioned in the Old Testament in the *KJV*:
- Bashan-havoth-jair in Deuteronomy 3:14
- Chephar-haammonai in Joshua 18:24
- Kibroth-hattaavah in Numbers 11:34
- Sela-hammahlekoth in 1 Samuel 23:28

✣ **LONGEST WORD**

The five longest words in the *KJV* of the Bible, excluding place names and people are:
- unrighteousness, 22 times
- covenantbreakers, once
- unprofitableness, once
- evilfavoredness, once
- lovingkindnesses, four times

'Lovingkindnesses' comes twice in one verse: 'I will mention the lovingkindnesses of the LORD, and the praises of the LORD, according to all that the LORD hath bestowed on us, and the great goodness toward the

✣ **LONGEST TIME WITH NO BIBLE BOOKS BEING WRITTEN**

The gap between the last written Old Testament book (Malachi) and the first of the New Testament writings (probably Mark's Gospel) was 400 years. This 'silence' is called the Intertestamental Period.

✣ **GREATEST FAITH PUT IN THE OLD TESTAMENT**

Jesus quoted from 19 books of the Old Testament and referred to 20 Old Testament characters. The New Testament includes approximately 263 quotations from the Old Testament; and approximately 376 other references to the Old Testament.

GENESIS — God's creation to the patriarchs of Israel

EXODUS — Moses leads the Israelites out of slavery in Egypt

LEVITICUS — The Law explained

NUMBERS — Israel counted in the wilderness

DEUTERONOMY — God saves and blesses his chosen people

JOSHUA — Israel invades Canaan

JUDGES — The lawless period after the invasion of Canaan

RUTH — Blessing through faith

THE PENTATEUCH   **HISTORY**

✣ **MOST FREQUENTLY MENTIONED PERSON**

In the New Testament, in the *NIV*, 'Jesus' occurs 1,251 times, and 'Christ' 545 times. In the Old Testament, in the *NIV*, 'David' occurs 1,007 times and 57 times in the New Testament.

ANIMALS

✣ **MOST MENTIONED**

The most mentioned animal in the Bible is the sheep. The word 'sheep' comes 200 times and 'lamb' 188 times in the *KJV*.

CROPS

✣ **MOST MENTIONED IN NEW TESTAMENT**

Figs are mentioned 21 times in the New Testament.

house of Israel, which he hath bestowed on them according to his mercies, and according to the multitude of his lovingkindnesses.'
ISAIAH 63:7, *KJV*.

✣ **ODDEST NAME**

A person named 'Dodo' is mentioned in Judges 10:1.

✣ **MOST MENTIONED IN OLD TESTAMENT**

Corn is mentioned 86 times in the Old Testament.

1 SAMUEL	The last of the great judges
2 SAMUEL	David's reign as king of Israel
1 KINGS	The history of the Israelite monarchy
2 KINGS	The history of the divided kingdom
1 CHRONICLES	God still keeps his promises to the nation
2 CHRONICLES	From King Solomon to the fall of Jerusalem
EZRA	The return to Jerusalem from exile in Babylon
NEHEMIAH	Rebuilding the walls and the relationship with God
ESTHER	God's people saved from destruction
JOB	Challenging God
PSALMS	The Hymn and prayer book of the Bible
PROVERBS	A collection of moral and religious teachings
ECCLESIASTES	The thoughts of 'the Philosopher'
SONG OF SONGS	A collection of love poems
ISAIAH	Warning, hope and reassurance

HISTORY (continued)   **POETRY & WISDOM**   **PROPHETS**

UNUSUAL HAPPENINGS

✠ LONGEST CHANT

An Ephesian mob chanted for two hours, 'Great is Artemis of the Ephesians!' (Acts 19:34).

✠ PEOPLE KILLED BECAUSE OF THE LETTERS 'SH'

42,000 Ephraimites were killed in the time of the Judges because they could not pronounce the sound 'sh' at the start of the word 'Shibboleth' (Judges 12:6).

✠ LONGEST DAY

'The sun stopped in the middle of the sky and delayed going down about a full day' (Joshua 10:13).

✠ TALKING DONKEY

Balaam was spoken to by a donkey in Numbers 22:28-30.

✠ BIGGEST BED

Og, king of Bashan, had an iron bed that was more than 13 feet long and 6 feet wide. See Deuteronomy 3:11.

FIRSTS IN THE BIBLE

✠ FIRST MESSIANIC PROPHECY

The first messianic prophecy in the Bible, the good news of a redeemer, comes in Genesis 3:15.

✠ FIRST MENTION OF BELIEVING

'Abram believed the LORD, and he credited it to him as righteousness' (Genesis 15:6).

✠ FIRST POLYGAMIST

'Lamech married two women, one named Adah and the other Zillah' (Genesis 4:19).

✠ FIRST SON DYING BEFORE HIS FATHER

'While they were in the field, Cain attacked his brother Abel and killed him' (Genesis 4:8).

JEREMIAH	LAMENTATIONS	EZEKIEL	DANIEL	HOSEA	JOEL	AMOS	OBADIAH	JONAH	MICAH	NAHUM	HABAKKUK	ZEPHANIAH	HAGGAI	ZECHARIAH	MALACHI
Prophecies of judgement, exile and restoration	Poems lamenting the destruction of Jerusalem	Prophecies of judgement, destruction of Jerusalem	Stories and visions bring hope to God's people	Emphasizing the need for inner renewal	Prophecies against idolatry and faithlessness	A call to repent and receive God's blessing	A call for justice	Prophecies of punishment for Israel's enemies	The reluctant prophet	Signs of hope	Celebrating the fall of Nineveh	Prophecies of doom for the unrighteous	Israel's doom and redemption	Urging the people to rebuild the Temple	Messages of waring, hope, prosperity and peace	A call to Israel to renew their covenant with God

PROPHETS (continued)

▶▶

✤ FIRST RAINBOW
'I have set my rainbow in the clouds, and it will be the sign of the covenant between me and the earth' (Genesis 9:13).

✤ FIRST PARABLE
The first parable recorded in the Bible comes in Judges 9:8-15 and is about 'the trees [who] went out to anoint a king for themselves.'

✤ FIRST AND LAST 'I WILL'
Both speak of close relationships. 'I will make a helper suitable for him' (Genesis 2:18). 'Come, I will show you the bride, the wife of the Lamb' (Revelation 21:9).

✤ FIRST CHRISTIAN SERMON
Peter preached the first Christian sermon on the Day of Pentecost, when 'about three thousand were added to their number that day' (Acts 2:14-41).

✤ FIRST COMMANDMENT
The first commandment from the Ten Commandments is: 'You shall have no other gods before me' (Exodus 20:3).

"Ah ... the smallest tribe!"

SMALLEST

✤ SMALLEST TRIBE OF ISRAEL
Benjamin was the smallest tribe of Israel. (1 Samuel 9:21).

✤ SHORTEST PRAYER
The disciples prayed, 'Lord, save us!' (Matthew 8:25).

MOST FREQUENT WORD

✤ 'THE'
In the *KJV* the word 'the' occurs 63,924 times.

MATTHEW	MARK	LUKE	JOHN	ACTS	ROMANS	1 CORINTHIANS	2 CORINTHIANS	GALATIANS	EPHESIANS	PHILIPPIANS	COLOSSIANS	1 THESSALONIANS	2 THESSALONIANS	1 TIMOTHY
Jesus the great teacher	Jesus the man of action	Jesus the promised Savior	Jesus the eternal Word of God	The story of the early church	All humankind needs to be put right with God	Dealing with the problems of the Christian life	Paul asserts his authority as an apostle	Paul writes against false teachings	The oneness of God's people in union with Christ	Encouragement and confidence in time of trouble	Full salvation through Jesus Christ alone	A letter of encouragement and reassurance	Remain steady in your faith	Warnings, instructions and advice to a young Christian

GOSPELS & ACTS   **LETTERS**

SECOND MOST FREQUENT WORD

The second most frequently occurring word in the Bible is the word 'and.' Before the days of computers Thomas Hartwell Horne, 1780-1862, tried to count the number of times 'and' occurs in the Bible. He made it 46,227 times, but managed to miss out over 5,000 occurrences of the word. In the *KJV* 'and' appears 51,696 times.

SURVIVING COPIES

FIRST PEOPLE TO MAKE WIDE USE OF THE CODEX

Because Christians wanted to read their Scriptures in a more manageable form than rolls of papyrus, they were probably the first people to make extensive use of the codex – a bound book.

OLDEST HAND-WRITTEN BOOK

The oldest surviving hand-written book that is still in one piece dates back to about 1600 and is a Coptic Psalter. It was discovered at Beni Suef, Egypt, in 1984.

The Codex Sinaiticus.

FIRST REFERENCE TO ALL THE NEW TESTAMENT BOOKS

Emperor Constantine, after he had proclaimed Christianity a legal religion in AD 324, asked Eusebius of Caesarea to produce 50 copies of the Scriptures for use in Constantinople. Eusebius therefore collected into one volume, for the first time, all the writings of the New Testament.

2 TIMOTHY
More advice for a young Christian
TITUS
Advice regarding church leaders and conduct
PHILEMON
An appeal for reconciliation
HEBREWS
Jesus Christ is the true and final revelatioon of God
JAMES
Practical instructions to God's people
1 PETER
Encouragement for those facing persecution
2 PETER
Combating the work of false teachers
1 JOHN
Encouragement and warning
2 JOHN
An appeal to love one another
3 JOHN
A word of praise and warning
JUDE
A warning against false teachers
REVELATION
Visions of hope and encouragement

LETTERS (continued)

REVELATION

1.2 DISTRIBUTION

It is a well-known fact that the Bible is the world's best-selling book, even if only a fraction of the copies sold and distributed are actually read. The work of different Bible societies and organizations takes center stage in this section.

✛ **OLDEST PUBLISHER OF BIBLES**
The UK's oldest publisher of Bibles is the *Cambridge University Press*. The first Bible they published was the *Geneva Bible* in 1591. (See page 23.)

✛ **LARGEST DISTRIBUTOR OF CHRISTIAN LITERATURE IN NEPAL**
Gospel for Asia is the largest producer and distributor of Gospel literature in Nepal, and one of the largest in India with more than 136 million pieces of literature delivered since 1993. They have two huge trucks that continually crisscross India, taking literature to regional warehouses for the use of local Christians.

THE BIBLE SOCIETIES

✛ **MOST INFLUENTIAL 25-MILE WALK**
The story is told of a 15-year-old girl, Mary Jones, from the Welsh village of Llanfihangel-y-Pennant, who spent six years saving up to buy a Bible. But there were no Bibles to be bought in her village so Mary Jones had to walk to Bala, over 25 miles away, where Bibles could be purchased from the Rev Charles. As a result of this experience, in December 1802, the Rev Charles told a committee of the *Religious Tract Society* about the desperate need for Bibles in the Welsh language giving the example of Mary Jones. On March 7, 1804, the *British and Foreign Bible Society* was formed 'for the wider distribution of the Scriptures, without note or comment.'

By 1907, the *BFBS* had distributed 203,931,768 Bibles, Testaments and portions of Scripture throughout the world. Between 1816 and 1975 *The Bible Society* distributed 2,458,000,000 Bibles.

The Bible Mary Jones bought is now in the Cambridge University Library.

GIDEONS

✠ OLDEST AMERICAN CHRISTIAN BUSINESS AND PROFESSIONAL MEN'S ASSOCIATION

The *Gideons International*, founded on July 1, 1899, by Samuel E. Hill (1867-1936), John H. Nicholson (1859-1946) and William J. Knights (1853-1940) serves as an extended missionary arm of the church and is the oldest Christian business and professional men's association in the United States of America. The association has more than 130,000 members, located in over 170 countries.

✠ BIGGEST PLACEMENT OF BIBLES

The *Gideons International* first placed Bibles in hotels in 1908. It now distributes Bibles to hotel rooms, hospitals and prisons. Every year the association places and distributes more than 45,000,000 Scriptures worldwide.

✠ ONLY AMERICAN SUPREME COURT CHIEF OF JUSTICE TO FOUND A BIBLE SOCIETY

John Adams, second President of the US and first Vice-President under George Washington, founded the American Bible Society.

On February 22, 1756, he wrote in his personal diary: 'Suppose a nation in some distant region should take the Bible for their only law book, and every member should regulate his conduct by the precepts there exhibited! Every member would be obliged in conscience, to temperance, frugality, and industry; to justice, kindness, and charity toward his fellow men; and to piety, love, and reverence toward Almighty God ... What a Utopia, what a Paradise this would be.'

UNITED BIBLE SOCIETIES

✠ HIGHEST TOTAL OF DISTRIBUTED SCRIPTURES

In 1997 the *United Bible Societies* distributed more Bibles than ever before – 20,035,360.

In addition to this they distributed: 18,553,174 New Testaments, and 456,517,465 selections (less than one book of the Bible). The overall total of Scriptures distributed by the *United Bible Societies* amounted to 561,633,376.

✠ RECORD NUMBER OF BIBLES FOR CHINA

Amity Press has printed over 15 million Bibles for China. They produced a record number in 1998 – 2.1 million.

China, traditionally opposed to the Gospel, has a growing Christian presence.

1.3 TRANSLATIONS

Wouldn't it be wonderful if the day should dawn when everyone could read the Bible in his or her own language? This section charts the progress of different translations of the Bible. Printed Scriptures are now available in the mother tongue of nearly 99% of the world's population. This unprecedented feat marks the greatest achievement in the history of written communications.

The story of the building of the tower of Babel in Genesis 11 marks the beginning of languages. The tower may well have been a ziggurat, similar to this artist's impression of the temple of the moon-god at Ur.

EARLY TRANSLATIONS

✣ 72 INDEPENDENT, IDENTICAL TRANSLATIONS
The *Septuagint* (usually written *LXX*) is the Greek translation of the Hebrew Old Testament which was developed in Alexandria, Egypt. Tradition maintains that in the 3rd century BC, 70 (or 72) translators worked alone in individual cells and when they compared their work, their translations were exactly the same. Many thought that the *Septuagint* was divinely inspired. The New Testament writers sometimes quoted from the *Septuagint* translation.

✣ 1,000 YEAR LEGACY
Jerome, one of the the most learned men of the 4th century, was asked by Pope Damasus to produce a revision of existing, inedequate, Latin texts of the Bible. Having taken Hebrew lessons, Jerome made a translation of the Old Testament, working directly from the Hebrew, and not from the *Septuagint*. His translation of the Old and New Testaments, which became known as the *Vulgate*, had a major influence on the liturgy and theology of Europe for 1,000 years.

TRANSLATORS

✣ THE MOST FAMOUS ALPHABET
The most famous alphabet developed by Christian missionaries was the Cyrillic alphabet. Cyril and Methodus, two brothers, went as missionaries to the Slavic people in the 9th century. Cyril wanted to translate the Bible for the Slavic people, but they had no alphabet. So he invented an alphabet especially for them. He mostly used Greek letters, but also some Armenian and Hebrew letters, as well as some letters he made up himself. The Cyrillic alphabet is still used in Russia, Bulgaria and Serbia.

NUMBER OF BIBLE TRANSLATIONS

✠ OVERVIEW OF SCRIPTURE TRANSLATION

AD 100	Translated into 6 languages
200	Translated into 7 languages
300	Translated into 9 languages
400	Translated into 11 languages
500	Translated into 13 languages
600	Translated into 14 languages
700	Translated into 15 languages
900	Translated into 16 languages
1000	Translated into 17 languages
1100	Translated into 19 languages
1200	Translated into 22 languages
1300	Translated into 26 languages
1400	Translated into 30 languages
1500	Translated into 34 languages
1600	Translated into 38 languages
1700	Translated into 52 languages
1800	Translated into 67 languages
1900	Translated into 537 languages
2000	Translated into 2,233 languages

✠ GROUP OF LANGUAGES WITH MOST BIBLE TRANSLATIONS

There are nearly 600 translations of the Bible in African languages and dialects. This is the largest single group of languages into which the Bible has been translated.

✠ THE GREATEST NUMBER OF BIBLE TRANSLATIONS

By 1998 the number of languages having at least a portion of the Bible reached 2,197. That is 30 more languages than in 1997.

✠ STATISTICAL SUMMARY OF LANGUAGES WITH SCRIPTURES

CONTINENT/REGION	PORTIONS	NEW TESTAMENT	BIBLES	TOTALS
Africa	227	254	136	617
Asia	228	203	111	542
Australasia	179	175	30	384
Europe	107	28	62	197
North America	45	23	7	75
Caribbean/Latin America	141	222	16	379
Constructed languages	2	0	1	3
Totals:	929	905	363	2197

✠ EX-COBBLER'S TRANSLATION OF THE BIBLE INTO 36 LANGUAGES

William Carey (1761-1834) left school at age 14 and became a cobbler. Later he became a renowned missionary and is still known by the title – 'the father of modern missions.' He oversaw the translation of the Bible into over 36 languages while himself-translating the Bible into 34 Asian languages.

DIFFERENT LANGUAGES

✠ THE BIBLE INTO ENGLISH

Although there were some early translations of parts of the Bible into Anglo Saxon and local dialects, the first translation of the entire Bible into an English that most people could understand was made in the late 14th century by the followers of Wycliffe. This translation was based on the Latin *Vulgate*.

✤ FIRST PUBLICATION OF GREEK NEW TESTAMENT

The Basle firm of Froben in Switzerland published the New Testament in Greek in 1516. It was prepared by the great Dutch scholar Desiderius Erasmus. In his preface Erasmus wrote: 'I could wish that every woman might read the Gospel and the Epistles of St Paul. Would that these were translated into each and every language so that they might be read and understood not only by the Scots and Irishmen, but also by Turks and Saracens ... Would that the farmer might sing snatches of Scripture at his plow and that the weaver might hum phrases of Scripture to the tune of his shuttle, that the traveler might lighten with stories from Scripture the weariness of his journey.'

✤ FIRST ENGLISH NEW TESTAMENT TRANSLATION USING GREEK MANUSCRIPTS

In Wycliffe's day it was illegal to have the Bible in English. People were even burned for teaching their children the Apostles' Creed, the Lord's Prayer, and the Ten Commandments in English.

Tyndale left England in order to translate the Bible. His New Testament, which was the first translation of the Bible from the original Greek into English was printed in 1525 and smuggled back into England.

✤ EARLIEST GERMANIC WRITING

The earliest known examples of writing in any Germanic language are fragments of a very early Bible translated by Ulfilas in the 4th century. Ulfilas (which means 'little wolf') spoke Greek and Latin in addition to his native Gothic and so was ideally suited to be a missionary to the barbarian tribes. Because the Goths did not then have any written language, before starting on his translation, Ulfilas devised the Gothic alphabet.

✤ BEST-KNOWN GERMAN TRANSLATION

Using the Hebrew Old Testament and Erasmus' Greek New Testament, Martin Luther produced a translation of the Bible in German. The whole Bible was published in Wittenberg in 1534.

✤ FIRST BOOK PRINTED IN AMERICA

The earliest Puritans did not sing hymns in their worship services but instead sang psalms or paraphrases of other Scriptures. Interestingly, the first book printed in America – the *Whole Book of Psalms*, also known as the *Bay Psalm Book* – was a metrical version of the psalms. This version was published in 1640.

✤ FIRST AMERICAN BIBLE

The Puritan John Eliot translated the Bible into Algonquian for the benefit of the North American Indians. Published in 1663, this translation was the first Bible to be printed in America.

✤ MUGWUMP BIBLE

Mugwump, an Algonquian word meaning 'great chief,' was used by Eliot to describe leaders such as Joshua or Gideon. It passed into the American language and now means any independent person, especially in the realm of politics.

✤ FIRST SPANISH BIBLE

The first complete Spanish Bible was published in Basle in 1569. It was the work of a former monk, Cassiodoro de Reina.

UNUSUAL BIBLES

✤ MOST BEAUTIFULLY-ILLUMINATED FOUR GOSPELS

The Book of Kells was produced around AD 800 and is one of the most beautifully illuminated manuscripts in the world. Written on vellum, it contains a Latin text of the four Gospels preceded by prefaces, summaries, and canon tables or concordances of Gospel passages. Throughout the text there are magnificent and intricate whole pages of decoration as well as smaller painted decorations. The manuscript was given to Trinity College Dublin in the 17th century.

Opposite: the start of the Gospel of John from *The Book of Kells*, 8th-9th century.

PRINTING OF BIBLES

✠ FIRST BIBLE PRINTED BY MOVABLE TYPE

In 1456 Johann Gutenberg produced the first printed Bible. It became the first complete book printed in the western hemisphere. Gutenberg used several hundred pieces of movable type and assembled them on to metal sheets. Ink was then placed on the type and the paper was pressed to the type. The impression became the printed words read by the reader.

Engraving of an early hand-operated printing press.

✠ MOST EXPENSIVE PRINTED BOOK

On October 22, 1987, a copy of the Old Testament containing Genesis through Psalms, printed in 1455, was sold at Christie's Auction House in New York City for $5.39 million.

✠ SMALLEST BIBLE

The 'mite' Bible, the smallest in the world, measured 1 3/4 in by 1 1/4 in. Its 936 pages included illustrations by C.B. Birch ARA. It was bound in leather, with flaps and a magnifier.

✠ BIBLE GIVEN THE MOST NUMBER OF NAMES

The 'Great' Bible, printed in 1539, was so called because of the size of its pages, which measured 9 in by 15 in. It was also called *Cromwell's Bible* because of the support Cromwell gave to its production. The 1540 edition included an introduction written by Archbishop Cranmer and is therefore sometimes known as *Cranmer's Bible*. In 1541 King Henry VIII ordered that a copy of the *Great Bible* be chained to a reading desk in the front of every parish church in England, resulting in it being known at times as the *Chained Bible*.

EARLIEST COPIES

✠ EARLIEST SURVIVING PART OF A NEW TESTAMENT BOOK

The earliest surviving fragment of a New Testament book is a papyrus fragment containing John 18:31-33, 37ff. It was written in Greek and the handwriting dates it to AD 125-150. Known as P52, it was found in Egypt, and is now housed in the Rylands Library at Manchester, England.

BIBLES WITH MISPRINTS

✠ 'WICKED' BIBLE

In 1631 an English Bible printer forgot the 'not' in one of the Ten Commandments. His version of Exodus 20:14 reads: 'Thou shalt commit adultery.' This edition of the Bible became known as the *Wicked Bible*, and the printer had to pay a large fine of £300. King Charles I commanded that all copies of this Bible be destroyed.

✠ 'BUG' BIBLE

Coverdale's translation of Psalm 91:5 reads: 'Thou shalt not nede to be afrayed for eny bugges by night.'

✠ 'ACHING' BIBLE

Two missing letters once cost *Oxford Press* two guineas. Two readers independently found that Matthew 26:55 was printed,

'Christ was aching in the Temple,' and were given a guinea each for their discovery.

✠ 'TREACLE' BIBLE
The *Bishop's Bible* of 1569, a revision of Miles Coverdale's translation of the Bible (mainly undertaken by bishops), translated Jeremiah 8:22 as, 'There is no triacle at Galaad.'

✠ 'PLACE-MAKER'S' BIBLE
The *Geneva Bible* of 1562 misprinted Matthew 5:9 as, 'Blessed are the place-makers.' This was a translation of the Bible prepared by a group of English Protestants living in Geneva, in exile from the persecutions of Protestants by Queen Mary.

✠ 'SNOWSHOES' BIBLE
In the translation for the Mumac Indians of Nova Scotia, Matthew 24:7 reads, 'A pair of *snowshoes* shall rise against a pair of *snowshoes*,' instead of reading, '*Nation* shall rise against *nation*,' The difference was made by the misplacement of one letter: '*naookt*u*kumiksijik*,' means *nation*, whilst '*naookt*a*kumiksijik*,' means *snowshoe*.

✠ 'UNRIGHTEOUS' BIBLE
An edition of the Bible printed in Cambridge in 1653 contained the following error: 'Know ye not that the unrighteous shall inherit the kingdom of God?' (1 Corinthians 6:9).

✠ 'PALM LEAF' BIBLE
The library of the University of Gottingen, a town in central Germany, has a Bible written on 2,470 palm leaves.

✠ MISSIONARY BIBLES
Carey's Indian translations of the Bible, and Morrison's Chinese Bible are sometimes called 'missionary' Bibles.

✠ 'PRINTERS' BIBLE
The '*Printers*' *Bible* in 1702 replaced the word 'princes,' with 'printers,' so Psalm 119:161 read, 'Printers have persecuted me.'

✠ 'GOOD LUCK' BIBLE
Coverdale translated Psalm 129:8 as, 'We wish you good luck in the name of the Lord.'

✠ 'BREECHES' BIBLE
The *Geneva Bible*, first published in 1560, was called the '*Breeches*' *Bible* by booksellers because of the unusual way in which it translated Genesis 3:7: 'They sewed fig leaves together and made themselves breeches.'

✠ 'HE' BIBLE
The first edition of the *King James Version*, printed by Robert Barker early in 1611, is sometimes referred to as the '*He*' *Bible* because of its translation of Ruth 3:15 as, '... he went into the city.'

✠ 'MURDERER'S' BIBLE
In 1801 the '*Murderer's*' *Bible* declared, 'These are the murderers' (instead of 'murmurers'). See Numbers 17:5.

✠ 'VINEGAR' BIBLE
A Bible printed in 1717 had the heading at Luke 20, 'The Parable of the Vinegar,' instead of 'Vineyard.'

BIBLE COMMENTATORS

✠ FIRST BIBLE TO HAVE MARGINAL NOTES DATING BIBLICAL EVENTS
The edition of the *King James Version* of the Bible published in 1701 by Bishop William Lloyd was the first Bible to include marginal notes that dated biblical events in relation to the birth of Jesus.

✠ GREATEST BIBLE COMMENTATOR
John Calvin, 1509-64, the supreme Bible teacher of the Reformation era, ranks as one of the greatest Bible commentators of all time. He employed five secretaries to write down his lectures and he published detailed commentaries on all the books of the Bible except for the book of Revelation.

BIBLE VERSIONS

The following list gives some of the famous versions of the 20th century:

Initials	Name of Bible version	Date of first publication
CBW	Charles B. Williams (paraphrase)	1937 (New Testament only)
RSV	Revised Standard Version	1946 (New Testament)
		1952 (Old Testament)
JBP	J.B. Phillips (paraphrase)	1958 (Revised 1972)
AB	Amplified Bible	1958 (New Testament)
		1964 (Old Testament)
NASB	New American Standard Bible	1960 (New Testament)
		1971 (Old Testament)
JB	Jerusalem Bible	1966
GNB	Good News Bible	1966 (New Testament)
		1976 (Old Testament)
NEB	New English Bible	1970
LB	Living Bible (paraphrase)	1971
NIV	New International Version	1973 (New Testament)
		1978 (Old Testament)
NKJV	New King James Version	1979 (New Testament)
		1982 (Old Testament)
NJB	New Jerusalem Bible (Revised JB)	1985
NRSV	New Revised Standard Version	1989
TM	The Message (paraphrase)	1996
NLT	New Living Translation	1996

SALES OF VERSIONS OF THE BIBLE IN AMERICA

Currently the *NIV* accounts for nearly 45% of all Bible sales. Sales of the *KJV* and the *NKJV* together account for nearly 40%. So all of the other Bible versions put together only account for 15% of Bible sales in America.

COMMENTARIES

Calvin was the first person to comment on the Bible, verse by verse, in the way Bible commentaries do today.

Calvin commenting on
1 John 4:11-12

11. *Dear friends*. The apostle now urges us by God's example to *love one another*. Paul, too, sets Christ before us as offering himself to the Father as a fragrant sacrifice so that each of us might labor to benefit our neighbors (Ephesians 5:2). And John reminds us that our love ought not to be mercenary: he tells us to love our neighbors as *God so loved us*; for we ought to remember that we have been loved freely. And doubtless when we think about our own advantage, or do good things for our friends, it is self-love, and not love to others.

12. *No one has ever seen God*. Here the apostle shows that the power of God is comprehended by us by faith and love, so as to know that we are his children and that he dwells in us.

However, he speaks first of love, when he says that God lives in us if we love one another; for his love is *made complete*, or really proved to be, in us then. It is like saying that God shows himself as present when by his Spirit he forms our hearts so that they entertain brotherly love. Since love is from the Spirit of God, we cannot truly and with a sincere heart love one another unless the Spirit gives us his power. In this way he testifies that he lives in us. But God lives in us by his Spirit; so then, by love we prove that we have God remaining in us. On the other hand, whoever boasts that he has God and does not love the brothers, his falsehood is proved by this one thing, because he separates God from himself.

John Calvin.

John Owen commenting on Hebrews 13:5

Keep your life free from the love of money and be content with what you have, because God has said, 'Never will I leave you; never will I forsake you.'

'Free from the love of money.' How we live is of great importance in our Christian lives. A guideline the apostle gives here is to 'keep your life free from the love of money,' literally, 'without love of money,' or without covetousness (see Luke 16:14; 1 Timothy 3:3; 2 Timothy 3:2). Covetousness is an inordinate desire to enjoy more money than we have, or than God is pleased to give us: 'People who want to get rich fall into temptation and a trap and into many foolish and harmful desires that plunge men into destruction. For the love of money is a root of all kinds of evil. Some people, eager for money, have wandered from the faith and pierced themselves with many griefs' (1 Timothy 6:9-10).

'Never will I leave you; never will I forsake you.' Literally, 'by no means ... nor ... by no means.' The force of the negative here is emphasized by three negative particles. The aim is to remove all objections

that fear and unbelief give rise to. 'Let people do what they will, let any circumstances arise, I will not at any time, on any occasion, for any reason, leave you, nor forsake you.'

Positive blessings are contained in these negative expressions. 'Never will I leave you.' This assures us of God's presence: 'whatever your state or condition I will never withdraw my presence from you.'

'Never will I forsake you' assures us of God's help, as the apostle emphasizes in the next verse: 'I will never allow you to be helpless in any trouble; my help will continue with you.'

J14690

1.4 ARCHEOLOGICAL DISCOVERIES

It's mainly in the present century that evidence has been unearthed using modern archeological tools and measuring equipment that provides some confirmation of the Bible story. These archeological discoveries confirm the historical accuracy of many events, places and customs recorded in the Bible.

An early 19th century impression of Babylon.

✠ FINDINGS ASSESSED

'The reader may rest assured that nothing has been found [by archeologists] to disturb a reasonable faith, and nothing has been discovered which can disprove a single theological doctrine. We no longer trouble ourselves with attempts to "harmonize" religion and science, or to "prove" the Bible. The Bible can stand for itself.'
WILLIAM F ALBRIGHT, 1891-1971,
AN AMERICAN ARCHEOLOGIST AND EDUCATOR
WITH A HIGHLY RESPECTED INTERNATIONAL REPU-
TATION FOR HIS EXCAVATIONS OF BIBLICAL SITES.

✠ THE IMPROBABLE SEEMS POSSIBLE

After they escaped from Egypt the Israelites made a tabernacle or 'worship tent.' They decorated it with about thirty talents of gold, that is, 900 kg/1,980 lbs. Tutankhamun's treasure, the most spectacular archeological discovery, demonstrates the wealth of Egypt and shows that great quantities of gold were available and used. Tutankhamun's solid gold inner coffin weighed 110kg/243lbs, so the amount of gold used in the tabernacle need not be any exaggeration. The escaping slaves used the gold that the Egyptians had given them (Exodus 12:36).

MAN-MADE STRUCTURES MENTIONED IN THE BIBLE AND UNEARTHED BY ARCHEOLOGISTS

✠ OLD TESTAMENT DISCOVERIES

- **The palace at Jericho** where Eglon, king of Moab, was assassinated by Ehud (Judges 3:12-30).
- **The royal palace at Samaria** where the kings of Israel lived (1 Kings 20:43; 21:1, 2; 22:39; 2 Kings 1:2; 15:25).
- 2 Kings 20:20 refers to '**the tunnel by which he [Hezekiah] brought water into the city [Jerusalem].**' In 1880 the Siloam inscription was discovered in Hezekiah's

1,777 foot long tunnel. It is a six-line inscription in classical Hebrew beautifully cut on the wall of the conduit about 19 feet from the Siloam end of the aqueduct. It records the completion of one of the most amazing engineering devices for water supply in the biblical period when workmen with wedge, hammer and pickax, digging from opposite ends, finally met.

- The royal palace in Babylon where King Belshazzar held the feast and Daniel interpreted the handwriting on the wall (Daniel 5).
- The royal palace in Susa where Esther was queen of the Persian king Xerxes (Esther 1:2; 2:3, 5, 9, 16).
- The royal gate at Susa where Mordecai, Esther's cousin, sat (Esther 2:19, 21; 3:2, 3; 4:2; 5:9, 13; 6:10, 12).

✤ THE OLDEST CITY IN THE WORLD

Dr Kathleen Kenyon, an archeologist, stated, 'Jericho can lay claim to being by far the oldest city in the world.' The Old Testament city of Jericho was founded at least 8,000 years ago. At Tell es-Sultan, the site of Old Testament Jericho, remains have been found of bee-hive-shaped 'round houses' which were the earliest form of Stone-Age house. Built by an oasis on the site of a perennial spring, Jericho became known as 'the city of palms.' It was the first city captured by Joshua and the invading Israelite army when they re-entered the promised land. Old Testament Jericho is a little to the north of the New Testament city which is the city of Jericho we know today.

✤ NEW TESTAMENT DISCOVERIES

- The foundation of the synagogue at Capernaum where Jesus cured a man with an unclean spirit (Mark 1:21-28).
- Jacob's well where Jesus spoke to the Samaritan woman (John 4).
- The Pool of Bethesda in Jerusalem, where Jesus healed a crippled man (John 5:1-14).
- The Pool of Siloam in Jerusalem, where Jesus healed a blind man (John 9:1-4).
- The theater at Ephesus where the riot of

Jericho is one of the oldest cities in the world. Scene of Joshua's first conquest in the Promised Land.

silversmiths occurred (Acts 19:29).
- Herod's palace at Caesarea where Paul was kept under guard (Acts 23:33-35).

HOW JESUS DIED

✤ CAVE TOMBS IN JERUSALEM

In 1968 a team of archeologists under the direction of V. Tzaferis discovered four cave-tombs at Giv'at ha-Mivtar (Ras el-Masaref), just north of Jerusalem near Mount Scopus.

The date of the tombs, revealed by the pottery dug up there, ranged from 180 BC to AD 70. These family tombs, hewn out of the soft limestone rock, with their branching chambers, date back to a Jewish cemetery of the time of Jesus.

✤ FIFTEEN OSSUARIES

Inside the caves 15 limestone ossuaries (small containers in which were kept the bones of deceased people) were unearthed. One of these skeletons was of a 24 to 28-year-old man who had been crucified. His name was scratched on his ossuary in letters 2 cm/1 inch high: Jehohanan.

✤ HANDS OR ARMS PIERCED?

The lower third of Jehohanan's right radial bone reveals a groove. This was likely to have been caused by the friction between a

Snow-capped mountains form a distant backcloth to the city of Baalbeck in Lebanon. These ruins are from the 1st century AD.

nail and the bone. Hence, his arms were nailed to the cross through the forearms and not through the wrists. His wrist bones were undamaged. It can possibly be deduced from this that Jesus' forearms, not hands, were pierced which is contrary to the customary portrayal of the death of Jesus in art.

✠ ONE NAIL FOR THE ANKLES

It was evident that Jehohanan's legs had been pressed together, bent, and twisted so that the calves were parallel to the horizontal section of the cross. His feet had been secured to the cross by a single iron nail driven simultaneously through both heels (*tuber calcanei*). With the iron nail were found the following: sediment, fragments of wood (Pistacia or Acacia), a limy crust, a portion of the right heel bone, a smaller piece of the left heel bone, and a fragment of olive wood. From this it is deduced that Jehohanan had been nailed to an olive wood cross with the right foot above the left and with his legs bent up double.

PHYSICAL REMAINS

✠ OSSUARY OF CAIAPHAS THE HIGH PRIEST

The first physical remains to be discovered of anyone mentioned in the Bible probably belong to Caiaphas who was high priest for 18 years. The Caiaphas family tomb was accidentally discovered by workers constructing a road in a park just south of the Old City of Jerusalem. A most beautifully decorated ossuary was inscribed with the name 'Joseph son of (or of the family of) Caiaphas.' Inside were the remains of a 60-year-old male, almost certainly those of the Caiaphas of the New Testament. Joseph, called Caiaphas, was high priest from AD 18 to 36.

A GREAT ARCHEOLOGICAL DISCOVERY – THE DEAD SEA SCROLLS

✠ CELEBRATED SHEPHERD BOY

In 1945 a shepherd boy, Muhammed ed Dhib, was looking for his sheep among the rocks near the Dead Sea. He threw a rock into a cave and heard jars shattering. After investigating he discovered clay jars stuffed with ancient manuscripts. As a result over 800 scrolls were found, dating from the 2nd century BC into the 1st century AD

Qumran: Cave of the Dead Sea Scrolls.

✠ LONGEST SCROLL

The Isaiah scroll is a copy of the book of Isaiah, written in Hebrew. It is a roll of leather 7.34 meters/24 feet long, 26 cm/10 inches wide. It consists of 17 sheets sewn together, with 54 columns of Hebrew writing.

Dead Sea scrolls. The Isiah Scroll, 1st century AD.

✠ MOST MANUSCRIPTS IN A SINGLE CAVE

In Cave number 4, 4,000 fragments of manuscripts which came from about 400 scrolls were discovered.

✠ OLDEST COPIES OF BIBLE BOOKS

Some of the Bible manuscripts among the Dead Sea Scrolls are close to 2,300 years old. Portions or complete copies of every book of the Old Testament, except Esther, have been found – making these almost 1,000 years older than the oldest copies of the Hebrew Old Testament previously known.

The Dead Sea Scrolls are the largest and oldest body of manuscripts relating to the Bible which have yet come to light. Shortly after they were discovered the historical, paleographic, and linguistic evidence, as well as carbon-14 dating, established that the scrolls were dated from the 3rd century BC to AD 68.

✠ GREATEST NUMBER OF MANUSCRIPTS

There are more manuscripts of the Bible on record than any other single book from the ancient world. More than 25,000 manuscripts of portions of the New Testament exist. Many of these are comparatively early manuscripts. Some are dated as early as AD 125-140.

When the surviving manuscripts concerning other ancient events are compared with the surviving Bible manuscripts, one can readily see just how good the Bible manuscripts are. Nobody doubts that Julius Caesar invaded Britain, but there are only ten ancient manuscripts that confirm this. The earliest of these were written about 800 years after the event.

Before the discovery of the Dead Sea Scrolls the earliest surviving copies of the Bible were about the same age (AD 900). The discovery of the Dead Sea Scrolls changed this dramatically.

BIBLE EVENTS

✠ **EVIDENCE FROM SOURCES OUTSIDE THE BIBLE ABOUT EVENTS MENTIONED IN THE BIBLE**

EVENT	BIBLE REFERENCE	REFERENCE OUTSIDE THE BIBLE
Campaign of the Assyrian King Sennacherib against Judah	2 Kings 18:13-16	**The Taylor Prism:** In the Annals of Sennacherib (705-681 BC) inscribed in clay on the Taylor Prism, the Assyrian monarch tells of his siege of Jerusalem (701 BC) in which he says that he shut up Hezekiah 'like a caged bird.' The Taylor Prism (also known as Sennacherib's Prism) is kept in the British Museum.
Siege of Lachish by Sennacherib	2 Kings 18:14, 17	**The Lachish letters:** Excavated at Lachish these 18 'letters' were found to have been written in Hebrew in the early 6th century BC. They were messages written on pieces of pottery (potsherds) containing information of political and military situations before the destruction of Jerusalem by Nebuchadnezzar.
Fall of Jerusalem to Nebuchadnezzar, King of Babylon	2 Kings 24:10-14	**The Babylonian Chronicles:** The Babylonian Chronicle for 605-594 is a clay tablet inscribed with a description of the battle of Carchemish (2 Chronicles 35:20). It states that Zedekiah was enthroned in King Jehoiachin's palace (2 Kings 24:17) and gives March 16, 579 BC as the date for Jerusalem's capture in Nebuchadnezzar's first siege.
King Mesha's revolt	2 Kings 3:4-5	**The Moabite Stone:** In 1886 in Diban (of Moab) an inscription on a block of stone, four feet high, two feet wide and one foot deep, was found. Part of the record states: 'I, Mesha, King of Moab, made this monument to Chemosh (god of Moab) to commemorate my deliverance from Israel. Omri, king of Israel, oppressed Moab, and his son (Ahab) after him.'
Freeing of the captives in Babylon by Cyrus the Great	Ezra 1:1-4; 6:3-4	**The Cyrus Cylinder:** This ten-inch clay cylinder inscribed with cuneiform writing was discovered by H. Rassam in the 19th century and is now in the British Museum in London. It contains the decree which Cyrus issued setting Israel free. Cyrus presents himself in the role of the 'liberator of the people,' and permitted the liberated captives to return to their original cities and practice their religion according to their own beliefs.

▶▶

✠ **MOST FAMOUS MAUSOLEUM OF A BIBLE PERSON**

The oldest mausoleum of a New Testament person belongs to Caesar Augustus. He erected it for himself on a grand scale in Rome. The remains exist today in the middle of the Piazza Augusto Imperatore. It was 285 feet in diameter and 143 feet high, and was surmounted by a statue of the emperor.

THE SETTING OF BIBLICAL ARCHEOLOGY

✠ **TALLEST MOUNTAIN IN PALESTINE**

The peak of Mt Hermon rises to 9,252 feet. The Mt Hermon range of mountains extends for 18 miles on the north-eastern border of Palestine. Mt Hermon is the probable site of the Transfiguration of Jesus (Mark 9:2-13).

EVENT	REFERENCE OUTSIDE THE BIBLE
The existence of Jesus	Recorded by Josephus, Suetonius, Tacitus, Thallus, Pliny the Younger, the Talmud, and Lucian

Josephus Josephus, a Jewish soldier and historian, who lived from AD 37 to about AD 100, wrote: 'At that time lived Jesus, a wise man, if he may be called a man, for he performed many wonderful works. He was a teacher of such men as received the truth with pleasure. He drew over to him many Jews and Gentiles. This was the Christ; and when Pilate, at the instigation of the chief men among us, had condemned him to the cross, they who before had conceived an affection for him, did not cease to adhere to him; for, on the third day, he appeared to them alive again, the divine prophets having foretold these and many wonderful things concerning him. And the sect of the Christians, so called from him, has not yet died out.'

Tacitus Tacitus, a 2nd-century Roman historian wrote: 'Nero punished with the utmost refinement of cruelty, a class hated for their abominations, who were commonly called Christians. Chrestus, from whom their name derived, was executed at the hands of the Procurator Pontius Pilate in the reign of Tiberius.'

✤ THE BIBLE'S AUTHENTICITY COMPARED WITH THE AUTHENTICITY OF OTHER ANCIENT WRITINGS

AUTHOR	DATE WRITTEN	EARLIEST COPY KNOWN	NUMBER OF COPIES
Caesar's Gallic Wars	100-44 BC	AD 900	10
Plato's Tetralogies	427-347 BC	AD 900	7
Tacitus	AD 100	AD 1100	20
Pliny the Younger	AD 61-113	AD 850	7
Thucydides	460-400 BC	AD 900	8
Sophocles	496-406 BC	AD 1000	100
Catullus	54 BC	AD 1550	3
Euripedes	480-406 BC	AD 1100	9
Aristotle	384-322 BC	AD 1100	5
The Bible	1500 BC - AD 95	AD 125	13,000

✤ THE LOWEST POINT ON THE EARTH'S SURFACE

The lowest point on the earth's surface is the Dead Sea (a large lake) covering an area of 393 square miles in the south of Palestine. The Dead Sea is 1,300 feet below sea level. Its maximum depth is 1,420 feet. The waters of the River Jordan, and of four wadis, flow into the sea and no water flows out of it. Yet the temperature in this deep rift valley is so warm that the water evaporates rapidly, leaving the sea level constant. Twenty-five per cent of the sea is salt (hence its biblical name Salt Sea) and the mineral level is so high that the Dead Sea supports no life. It is thought that the cities of Sodom and Gomorrah lie beneath its southern end. They were probably submerged when the land subsided as the result of a volcanic eruption.

.5 FIRST, LAST, GREATEST

This section concentrates on the different places in the Bible in which three familiar words or concepts appear: first, last and greatest. It's interesting to compare the first and the last commands of the risen Lord Jesus, and to observe who will be the first people to rise from the dead at Jesus' second coming.

'God called the light "day," and the darkness he called "night." And there was evening, and there was morning – the first day.'
GENESIS 1:5

FIRST

✠ **THE FIRST 'DAY' OF CREATION**
'God called the light "day," and the darkness he called "night." And there was evening, and there was morning – the first day' (Genesis 1:5).

✠ **FIRST MESSAGE AT JESUS' BIRTH**
'But the angel said to them [the shepherds], "Do not be afraid. I bring you good news of great joy that will be for all the people ..."' (Luke 2:10).

✠ **FIRST DISCIPLE**
Andrew. See John 1:40.

✠ **FIRST 'MISSIONARY'**
'The first thing Andrew did was to find his brother Simon and tell him, "We have found the Messiah" (that is, the Christ). And he brought him to Jesus' (John 1:41-42).

✠ **FIRST COMMANDMENT**
'Jesus said, "Love the Lord your God with all your passion and prayer and intelligence.' This is the most important [of God's commands], the first on any list' (Matthew 22:37-38, *The Message*).

✠ **THE SECOND COMMANDMENT**
'But there is a second [command of God] to set alongside it: "Love others as well as you love yourself"' (Matthew 22:39, *The Message*).

✠ **FIRST OF JESUS' MIRACULOUS SIGNS**
'This, [changing water into wine] the first of his miraculous signs, Jesus performed in Cana of Galilee' (John 2:11).

✠ **FIRST THING TO BE SOUGHT FOR**
'But seek first his kingdom and his righteousness, and all these things will be given you as well' (Matthew 6:33).

Jesus told the disciples that though they were fishermen he would make them 'fishers of men.'

✠ FIRST DISCIPLE TO REACH THE EMPTY TOMB

This was John, who never mentions himself by name in his Gospel. 'So Peter and the other disciple started for the tomb. Both were running, but the other disciple outran Peter and reached the tomb first' (John 20:3-4).

✠ FIRST PERSON TO SEE THE RISEN LORD

'Jesus said to her, "Mary." She turned towards him and cried out in Aramaic, "Raboni!" (which means Teacher) ... Mary Magdalene went to the disciples with the news: "I have seen the Lord!"' (John 20:16,18).

✠ FIRST COMMAND OF THE RISEN JESUS

'Go ... to my brothers and tell them...' (John 20:17).

✠ SECOND WORDS OF THE RISEN JESUS TO ALL THE DISCIPLES

'Peace be with you!' (Luke 24:36; John 20:19).

✠ FIRST COMMAND WITH A PROMISE

'"Honor your father and mother" – which is the first commandment with a promise' (Ephesians 6:2).

LAST

LAST COMMAND OF THE RISEN JESUS

'Therefore go and make disciples of all nations' (Matthew 28:19).

✛ THE LAST ENEMY

'The last enemy to be destroyed is death' (1 Corinthians 15:26).

✛ GOD'S LAST DAY

'For my Father's will is that everyone who looks to the Son and believes in him shall have eternal life, and I will raise him up at the last day'(John 6:40).

GREATEST

✛ GREATEST IN GOD'S KINGDOM

'I tell you the truth: Among those born of women there has not risen anyone greater than John the Baptist; yet he who is least in the kingdom of heaven is greater than he' (Matthew 11:11).

✛ GREATEST LOVE

'Greater love has no one than this, that he lay down his life for his friends' (John 15:13).

✛ LOVE IS THE GREATEST

'And now these three remain: faith, hope and love. But the greatest of these is love' (1 Corinthians 13:13).

✛ FIRST TIME JESUS' FOLLOWERS CALLED 'CHRISTIANS'

'The disciples were called Christians first at Antioch' (Acts 11:26).

✛ THE FIRST PEOPLE TO RISE AT JESUS' SECOND COMING

The first people to rise at Jesus' second coming will be those who have already died. 'For the Lord himself will come down from heaven, with a loud command, with the voice of the archangel and with the trumpet call of God and the dead in Christ will rise first' (1 Thessalonians 4:16).

Greater love … Jesus' sacrifice for us is remembered in the communion service.

Part 2

THE SPREAD OF CHRISTIANITY

2,000 YEARS – AN OVERVIEW

0-325
THE CHURCH MOVES OUT

14-37	Emperor Tiberius
29,30,33	Jesus' crucifixion, resurrection … the Church is born
43	Southern Britain conquered
44	Paul & Barnabas to Jerusalem on famine relief
49	End of Paul's 1st missionary journey
54-68	Emperor Nero
c.58-62	Paul imprisoned at Rome
60-100	Gospels and New Testament letters written
64	Great fire of Rome – Nero persecutes Christians
70	Jerusalem destroyed by Romans
73	Fall of Masada
81-96	Emperor Domitian, continued persecution of Christians
132-35	Bar Cochba revolt
135	Jews expelled from Jerusalem
144	Marcion excommunicated for heresy

c.155	Justin Martyr, *First Apology*
c.178-200	Irenaeus bishop of Lyons
202	Origen flees persecution to Alexandria
250	Persecution under Emperor Decius
258	Martyrdom of Cyprian, bishop of Carthage
303	Persecution under Diocletian begins
305	Antony of Egypt founds hermit colony
306-37	Emperor Constantine

325-600
CONQUEST

325	Council of Nicea settles Arian heresy – declares "Christ is one in essence with the Father"
350	Constantinople becomes 'New Rome'
374	Ambrose bishop of Milan
381	1st Council of Constantinople
386	Jerome to Bethlehem
395-430	Augustine Bishop of Hippo(N Africa)
405	Jerome completes translation of Scriptures into Latin (the Vulgate)
410	Goths sack Rome
416	Pelagius condemned at Council of Carthage
431	Council of Ephesus
430-60	Patrick in Ireland
455	Vandals overrun Rome
527-65	Emperor Justinian wins back North Africa from Vandals, Italy from Goths
553	2nd Council of Constantinople
590-604	Pope Gregory I
597	Augustine sets foot in England

600-1500
CHRISTIAN RULE

632	Muhammad dies
638	Arabs conquer Jerusalem
681	3rd Council of Constantinople
716	Boniface to Frisia
731	Bede completes Ecclesiastical History of the English People
754	Boniface martyred in Frisia
787	2nd Council of Nicea
c.790+	Vikings invade Europe
800	Charlemagne crowned by Pope Leo III as Holy Roman Emperor
863+	Moravia evangelized by Cyril and Methodius
871-99	Alfred the Great defeats Danes, Christian teaching promoted in England
909	Abbey of Cluny established
988	Russia adopts Christianity
996-1021	Egyptian Coptic Church persecuted
1000-1442	Spain conquered for Christianity
1009	Church of the Holy Sepulcher, Jerusalem, destroyed
1049-54	Papal reform under Pope Leo IX
1066	William the Conqueror crowned King of England
1071+	Seljuk Turks invade Holy Land
1073-85	Pope Gregory VII
1076	Council of Worms
1093+	Anselm Archbishop of Canterbury

1095	Urban II preaches 1st Crusade at Clermont
1098	Cistercian Order established at Citeaux
1099	Jerusalem reclaimed by Crusaders
1115+	Peter Abelard teaches at Paris
1115+	Bernard first abbot at Clairvaux (Citeaux)
1123	1st Lateran Council
1139	2nd Lateran Council
1146	Preaching of 2nd Crusade by Bernard
1147+	Universities founded at Oxford and Paris
1159	Schism in Rome under Emperor Barbarossa
1170	Archbishop Thomas à Becket murdered at Canterbury
1177	Barbarossa and Alexander III settle schism
1177	3rd Lateran Council
1187	Saladin captures Jerusalem
1189-92	3rd Crusade
1198-1216	Pope Innocent III
1204	4th Crusade diverted to Constantinople
1204	Latin Empire founded
1226	Francis of Assisi dies
1215	4th Lateran Council
1216	Dominican Friars established
1217-21	5th Crusade (Damietta)
1228-9	Jerusalem recovered by Frederick II
1232	Papal inquisition under Gregory IX

1244	Jerusalem reclaimed by Muslims
1245	1st Council of Lyon – Frederick II deposed
1250	Cologne Cathedral started
1261	Constantine recovered
1274	2nd Council of Lyon
1281-1924	Ottoman State
1291	Acre falls (last Crusader stronghold)
1302	Boniface VIII proclaims universal rule of the Pope
1305	Clement V elected Pope: French exile of papacy begins
1314	Dante's *Divine Comedy*
1327-47	William of Ockham rails against the papacy
1348-9	The Black Death
1375-82	John Wyclif attacks clerical wealth and papal authority
1378-1429	The Great Schism: two popes
1414-18	Council of Constance decrees general councils are superior to the Pope
1415	Jan Hus martyred
1418	Thomas á Kempis, *Imitation of Christ*
1423+	Portuguese voyages of discovery begin
1431-49	Council of Basle
1453	Constantinople overrun by Ottoman Turks
1479	Spanish Inquisition
1492	Muslims expelled from Spain
1498	Savonarola martyred in Florence

1508+	Michelangelo paints Sistine Chapel ceiling
1509	Erasmus attacks corruption in Church
1510	Martin Luther to Rome
1517	Luther's 95 theses nailed to Wittenberg church doors
1519	Hernando Cortés strikes Aztec empire, Mexico
1519	Zwingli to Zurich
1521	Martin Luther excommunicated
1521	Diet of Worms
1522-3	Ignatius Loyola, *Spiritual Exercises*
1523+	Rise of Anabaptists
1524	Franciscans in Mexico
1524-26	German Peasants' Revolt
1525	William Tyndale's New Testament published in Germany
1528	Reformation spreads
1529	Protestantism begins
1530	Diet of Augsburg
1534	Act of Supremacy (England)
1535	Thomas More executed
1536	John Calvin, *Institutes*

1539	Great Bible printed
1540+	Jesuit movement established
1542	Francis Xavier to India
1546	Council of Trent
1549	First Book of Common Prayer (England)
1555	Bishops Latimer and Ridley burnt at stake
1556	Archbishop Cranmer burnt
1560	Reformed Church established in Scotland
1572	Teresa of Avila receives mystical visions
1588	Spanish Armada defeated
1596-1650	René Descartes, founder of modern philosophy
1598	Edict of Nantes grants liberty to Protestants in France
1601	Matteo Ricci to Peking
1611	King James Bible published
1614	Christian worship prohibited in Japan
1618-48	Thirty Years' War
1620	Mayflower sets sail for America
1626	Jesuit Church established in Tibet
1632	Galileo Galilei introduces the idea of a revolving world
1633	Galileo forced to retract his ideas as heresy
1647+	George Foxe establishes Quaker movement

THE AGE OF REASON AND REVIVAL

1654	Blaise Pascal converted to Christianity
1660	Restoration of Charles II and the Anglican Church
1667	John Milton, *Paradise Lost*
1678	John Bunyan, *Pilgrim's Progress* Part 1
1682	William Penn founds Pennsylvania
1685	Louis XIV revokes Edict of Nantes
1689	Act of Toleration introduced (England)
1692	Christian worship allowed in China by imperial decree
1701	Foundation of the Society for the Propagation of the Gospel in Foreign Parts
1721	Peter the Great places Russian Church under State control
1722	Count Zinzendorf founds Pietist Herrnhut colony (Germany)
1723-6	Christian persecution in China
1723-50	J.S. Bach composes his great works at Leipzig
1724	Moravian Church established
1726	The 'Great Awakening' starts (N. America)
1727	Jonathan Edwards converted
1734	Voltaire, *Lettres Philosophiques*
1738	Conversion of John Wesley
1740-58	Pope Benedict XIV
1740	George Whitefield preaches in America
1742	Handel's *Messiah* first performed
1749+	Emanuel Swedenborg's mystical writings
1759	Quebec captured by British: Roman Catholics given free exercise of religion
1773	Jesuit Order suppressed by Pope Clement XIV
1783	Treaty of Versailles
1783	American Independence
1788	Slave trading regulated in Britain
1789	Church property in France to be sold

1789-1914
EMPIRE-BUILDING

1792	Baptist Missionary Society founded
1793-4	'Dechristianization' in France
1799	Church Missionary Society formed
1800	'Second Great Awakening' in America
1802	Napoleon Bonaparte's Concordat with Rome
1804	British and Foreign Bible Society formed
1805	Henry Martin travels as missionary to India
1809	Slave trade abolished in Britain
1810-24	Spanish American republics struggle for independence from Spain
1820	Zulu kingdom created
1821	Greeks revolt against Ottoman rule: Gregory Patriarch of Constantinople executed
1826-30+	Religious orders suppressed (South America)
1826	Widow-burning prohibited in British India
1833	Oxford Movement begins (England)
1833	Slavery abolished throughout British Empire
1839	Slavery condemned by Pope Gregory XVI
1840	David Livingstone to Africa
1843+	Kierkegaard introduces existentialism
1845	Baptists and Methodists in US South split from the North
1847	Brigham Young moves Mormon headquarters to Salt Lake City
1851	State support of religion ends in South Australia
1852	Holy Synod established in Greece
1854	Immaculate conception of the Virgin Mary becomes an article of Catholic faith
1857	Uprising and revolt in India
1858	Bernadette has visions at Lourdes
1858	Opium importation and entry of Christian missionaries imposed upon China
1859	Charles Darwin, *On the Origin of Species*
1865	Samuel Crowther first black bishop of Nigeria
1865	China Inland Mission founded
1867	1st Lambeth Conference, London
1869-70	1st Vatican Council: papal infallibility decreed

1914-
A MODERN WORLD

1871	Anglican Church disestablished in Ireland
1873	Persecution of Christians in Japan ended
1879-82	Lay education introduced in France
1889	Foundation of Rhodesia
1895	World Student Christian Federation begins
1898	First Protestant missionaries to Philippines
1900	Boxer Uprising (China)
1906-7	Separation of Church and State (France)
1910	Union of South Africa founded
1912	Australian Inland Mission (and Flying Doctor organization)

1914	Assemblies of God movement begins in North America
1914-18	First World War
1915	Einstein's General Theory of Relativity
1915	Klu Klux Klan born
1917	Russian Revolution begins
1918	New Russian Soviet government separates Church and State
1919	Karl Barth, *Commentary on Romans*
1924	Ottoman State dissolved
1928-30	Gandhi begins civil disobedience campaign against British rule (India)
1929	The Wall Street Crash leads to recession in the West
1929	'Apartheid' first coined in South Africa to describe racial segregation
1931	Spain declared a republic
1933	Adolf Hitler creates Nazi dictatorship (Germany)
1939-45	Second World War
1940	Brother Roger founds Taizé order
1941	Japanese attack on Pearl Harbor brings US into war
1943	Russian Orthodox Church and Stalin form concordat
1945	First nuclear bombs tested in New Mexico
1945	Atomic bombs on Japan force end of war in Pacific
1945	United Nations formed

1948	World Council of Churches formed
1948	Israel declared independent Zionist state
1949	Billy Graham begins evangelistic work
1951	All foreign missionaries removed from China
1951+	*The Theatre of the Absurd*, Samuel Becket
1958-64	Anti-Christian campaign in USSR under Kruschev
1959-65	Castro's Communist dictatorship in Cuba limits religious freedoms
1960	John F. Kennedy elected, first Catholic US president
1962-5	2nd Vatican Council
1964+	Clergy in Brazil stand against social injustice and abuse of human rights
1966	Pentecostal/charismatic movement adopted into mainline Christianity
1966	Cultural revolution (China): all Christian churches closed
1968	Papal encyclical *Humanae Vitaea* affirms Catholic Church's stance on birth control
1968	Rev Martin Luther King, civil rights campaigner, assassinated
1969	First landing on the moon
1977	'Born again' president Jimmy Carter's election heralds public relevance of evangelicalism

1979	Chinese churches reopened for public worship
1979	Liberation theology's excesses condemned by Pope John Paul II
1979	Mother Teresa awarded Nobel Peace Prize
1980	Archbishop Romero of El Salvador assassinated
1984+	The 'greenhouse effect' becomes global concern due to misuse of resources
1986	Churches help to bring down the Marcos regime in Philippines
1986	Desmond Tutu becomes Archbishop of Cape Town (South Africa)
1987-8	Tele-evangelist scandals in America
1989	Solidarity movement legalized in Poland
1989	Berlin Wall comes down
1989	Communism collapses in Czechoslovakia, E Germany
1990	Ordination of women accepted by Church of England
1990	'Ethnic cleansing' in former Yugoslavia condemned by churches
1993	Vatican establishes diplomatic relations with Israel for first time
1995	Reconciliation walk of apology for the Crusades by western Christians

2.1 FIRST APOSTLES

It is reputed that the apostles carried the Christian message to the far corners of the known world. Tradition says that Thomas became a missionary in India, and was martyred and buried in Mylapore, near Madras. Peter and Paul were martyred in Rome, the most important city in the civilized world. James, brother of John and son of Zebedee, is believed to have been the first Christian missionary to Spain. People still make pilgrimages to Santiago de Compostela, in northwestern Spain, where in the 9th century a shrine was discovered housing the reputed tomb of James.

When Jesus had called the Twelve together, he gave them power and authority to drive out all demons and to cure diseases, and he sent them out to preach the kingdom of God and to heal the sick. He told them: 'Take nothing for the journey — no staff, no bag, no bread, no money, no extra tunic. Whatever house you enter, stay there until you leave that town. If people do not welcome you, shake the dust off your feet when you leave their town, as a testimony against them.' So they set out and went from village to village, preaching the gospel and healing people everywhere.
LUKE 9:1-6

THE 12 APOSTLES

Jesus chose 12 of his disciples to be his apostles, 'those who are sent.' They accompanied Jesus on his three-year mission of teaching and healing.

✠ **ANDREW** *'manly'*
The first missionary. Andrew is sometimes thought of as the first 'missionary,' since he introduced his brother Simon to Jesus, just after he had met Jesus himself.

Andrew also spied the boy who had two fish and five barley loaves which Jesus used to feed 5,000 people.

The Gospels give us no details about the lives of:

✠ **BARTHOLOMEW** *'son of Talmai'*
Apart from his name appearing in the list of Jesus' 12 apostles given in Matthew, Mark and Luke and in Acts chapter one, the Bible says nothing about Bartholomew.

✠ **JUDAS** *'praise'*
All we know about this Judas is that he is to be distinguished from another disciple of the same name, 'not Iscariot.'

✠ **JAMES** (form of *Jacob*)
Apart from distinguishing him from another disciple of the same name, by calling him, 'son of Alphaeus,' the New Testament says nothing about this James.

✠ **JAMES** (form of *Jacob*)
James, and his more famous brother John, worked with their father Zebedee as fishermen in the family business. With Peter and John, James formed the inner circle of the three apostles who Jesus chose to share some of his most important earthly events, such as his transfiguration and his agony of prayer in Gethsemane.

✣ **JOHN** *'the Lord is gracious'*
John is the traditional author of the Gospel of John, as well as the book of Revelation and the three short letters of 1, 2, and 3 John. When Jesus was dying on the cross he asked John to look after Mary and become a son to her (John 19:26-27).

✣ **JUDAS ISCARIOT**
This Judas is forever remembered for his kiss of betrayal in the Garden of Gethsemane. John tells us that Judas was in charge of the apostles' money, but was a thief and helped himself from the money bag (John 12:6). He agreed to betray Jesus for a payment of 40 pieces of silver. Apart from the execution of James (the brother of John), Judas' suicide is the only recorded death of an apostle in the New Testament.

✣ **MATTHEW** *'gift of the Lord'*
As far as we know Matthew was the only member of the Twelve who worked for the Romans. As a tax-collector he would have been hated and regarded as a traitor for supporting the occupying foreign power. He is the writer of the first Gospel.

THOMAS *'Twin'*
After the crucifixion of Jesus, Thomas was the only member of the Twelve, apart from Judas Iscariot, who was not present when the apostles met together on the Sunday evening. Thomas doubted the resurrection of Jesus until he met the risen Lord Jesus for himself.

PHILIP *'lover of horses'*
As Andrew brought Peter to Jesus, so Philip brought Bartholomew (Nathanael) to Jesus. When Philip asked Jesus to show them the Father, Jesus said, 'Anyone who has seen me has seen the Father' (John 14:9).

SIMON *'hearing'*
Two of the 12 apostles had the name of Simon, one of them being known as Simon the Zealot. From this name it has been speculated that he may have been a member of

Jesus at table with his 12 apostles – a Last Supper scene by Cimabue.

the revolutionary group who were dedicated to driving out the Romans from Israel.

PETER *'rock'*
Jesus gave this Simon the name of Peter and Peter's name always heads the list of the 12 apostles: he was their hot-headed leader and spokesman. He is the only member of the Twelve to be told by Jesus how he would die: 'When you are old you will stretch out your hands' (John 21:18). This has been taken to mean that he would be martyred by crucifixion.

THE 'THIRTEENTH' APOSTLE

MATTHIAS
Matthias is the only apostle to join the Twelve after the death of Jesus. His appointment was made by prayer and the casting of lots (Acts 1:24,26), and he filled the gap left by Judas Iscariot.

Each century has seen the Christian gospel preached and taught by gifted men and women. Patrick preached in Ireland in the 5th century; in the following century Columba became the great missionary to Scotland; and, in the 8th century, Boniface left England to evangelize Germany. Boniface reformed the corrupt German church and has become known as the 'apostle to the Germans.' Individual missionaries, including some highly idiosyncratic but dedicated people, ventured into countries where none had previously dared to travel. In recent times we see the emergence of highly organized, global missionary organizations. They are all responding to the missionary command of Jesus: 'Go and make disciples of all nations' (Matthew 28:19).

✠ THE FIRST CHRISTIAN COUNTRY

In the 3rd century Armenia became the first officially Christian nation. Mesrop, bishop of Armenia (390-439), created an Armenian alphabet so the Bible could be translated into the language of his people.

✠ REJECTED BY A MISSIONARY SOCIETY

Despite being rejected by a missionary society, on Saturday, October 15, 1932, 30- year-old Gladys Aylward left Liverpool Street station in London with a one-way train ticket for China.

Aylward adopted China as her homeland, becoming a citizen in 1936. During the Sino-Chinese war, the courageous missionary led 100 children over the mountains on foot on a 100-mile journey to the safer province of Sian. At the end of the journey Aylward collapsed and doctors found that she was suffering from extreme exhaustion, malnutrition, typhus, and pneumonia.

Toward the end of her life, Gladys Aylward wrote: 'My heart is full of praise that one so insignificant, uneducated, and ordinary in every way could be used to his glory for the blessing of his people in poor persecuted China.'

Gladys Aylward.

A Lion attacks a Christian – Roman frieze.

SLAVES LIKENED TO ANGELS

Tradition says that Gregory the Great (c. 540-604), before he became pope, saw a group of young Anglo-Saxon slaves in the marketplace in Rome. When he enquired about them he was told that they were Angles. Gregory wanted them converted at once and said, 'non Angli, sed Angeli,' 'not Angles but angels.' When Gregory became pope he sent Augustine of Canterbury and 30 monks to evangelize England.

CHURCH GROWTH

MOST NUMBER OF CHURCHES BY THE END OF THE FIRST CENTURY

The country which had the largest number of churches at the end of Christianity's first century was Asia Minor (now Turkey), the scene of much of Paul's missionary work. The seven churches of Revelation 2-3 were all located in what is modern Turkey: Ephesus, Smyrna, Pergamum, Thyatira, Sardis, Philadelphia and Laodicea. (The word 'church' in the New Testament never refers to a building, but to a group of Christians who met together for prayer, worship and Bible study.)

RAPID GROWTH OF THE METHODIST CHURCH IN AMERICA

Between 1776 and 1850 the Methodists in America grew from being less than 3% of all church members in 1776 to more than 34%. This made them the largest religious body in the nation. They had 4,000 itinerant preachers, 8,000 local preachers and over a million members. At that time one in every 15 Americans was a Methodist.

GREATEST CHURCH GROWTH IN CHINA

It is estimated that between the Communist takeover in 1949 and the mid-1980s the church in China grew from 800,000 to an estimated 50 million. This ranks as one of the greatest surges of growth in all of Christian history.

EX-GRAVE-DIGGER MISSIONARIES

Count Nicolaus Ludwig von Zinzendorf, 1700-1760, and the Moravian Church, (which Zinzendorf refounded after a renewal took place at Herrnhut, Germany in 1722), began their first missionary outreach in 1732. This was to the slaves on the Danish island of St Thomas in the Virgin Islands and the first two missionaries were grave-diggers. The following year the Church sent a mission to Greenland. In 20 years they sent out more missionaries than all the Protestant missionary organizations had sent in the past 200 years.

In America the denomination was established in 1740 when it founded Bethlehem, Pennsylvania, which has remained the center of the Moravian Church in the US. There are over 55,000 Moravians in the US today.

MISSIONARY AVIATION FELLOWSHIP

✣ INSPIRED BY PILOTS FIGHTING IN WORLD WAR II

The purpose of *Missionary Aviation Fellowship* is to speed spiritual and physical care to people in places of deepest need, and to multiply the effectiveness of missions by using aviation and other strategic technologies. It was in the midst of World War II that God planted the seeds for what was to become the international ministry of the *Missionary Aviation Fellowship* (*MAF*). Pilots and navigators who had flown Allied planes in World War II were guided to use their skills in God's service to support humanitarian and missionary programs. The idea came about when a small group of Christian aviators listened to the harrowing travel experiences of a missionary serving in Borneo and realized that they could go where missionaries could seldom venture.

✣ FIRST *MAF* PILOT

The first operational flight was in 1946, when Betty Greene flew a Waco biplane on a mission to Mexico.

✣ THE LARGEST FLEET

Today, *MAF-US* serves in more than 48 countries worldwide. *MAF-US* alone logs nearly 80,000 flights a year to areas that canoe, mule, and camel can only reach with great difficulty, and places that can be cut off for up to half the year by rains. *MAF* operates and maintains the largest fleet of Cessna aircraft in the world. Each year more than 180 aircraft based in 30 countries make flights to over 3,000 destinations – mostly dirt airstrips in Africa, Asia, Eastern Europe, and Latin America. The flights carry dedicated teams bringing medical care, emergency food and Christian hope to countless thousands.

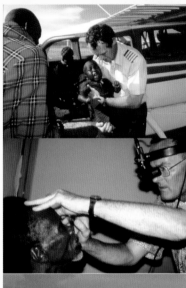

Northern Tanzania: taking a child for hospital attention to a snakebite.

Somalia: MAF aircraft are used to fly staff and specialist equipment into neighboring countries to give on-the-spot attention to eye problems.

Lake Victoria: the floatplane is used to link island-dwellers with missionaries and healthcare services.

Flying into southern Sudan, supporting a program to help combat the spread of tuberculosis.

✣ IT DIVISION

In 1994, *MAF-US* formed its Information Technology division and introduced e-mail services worldwide. Today, 69 e-mail hubs process over 3,000,000 messages each month.

LEADERS

✠ 'FASTEST' APPOINTMENT OF A BISHOP

Ambrose, 340-397, was appointed bishop of Milan one week after his baptism.

✠ FIRST AMERICAN WOMAN MISSIONARY

Ann Hasseltine Judson, 1789-1850, was the first American woman missionary to leave America and become a missionary. She worked in Burma where it took her 24 years to translate the Bible into Burmese and where she helped to establish 63 churches.

✠ FIRST ORDAINED WOMAN MINISTER

In 1853 Antoinette Brown Blackwell became the first American woman to be ordained a minister by a recognized denomination (Congregational).

✠ YOUNGEST ORDAINED PENTECOSTAL WOMAN PREACHER

Aimee Elizabeth Kennedy, 1890-1944, became the youngest ordained Pentecostal woman preacher when she was ordained in 1909. In 1921, she founded the International Church of the Foursquare Gospel. Its Angelus Temple in Los Angeles, California, attracted thousands of members who listened to Aimee preaching about divine faith healing and baptism in the Holy Spirit.

✠ FIRST WOMAN EPISCOPALIAN PRIEST

In 1977 Louise Brown became the first woman to be ordained a priest in the Episcopal Church. (The Episcopal Church is a Protestant Church governed by bishops. Outside the USA and Scotland it is known as the Anglican Church.)

✠ FIRST WOMAN BISHOP

In 1989 Barbara Harris became the first woman bishop in the Anglican/ Episcopalian Communion when she was consecrated Bishop of Boston.

✠ FIRST AFRICAN ANGLICAN BISHOP

Samuel Adjai Crowther, 1806-92, became the first African Anglican bishop in 1864.

✠ WORK IN RETIREMENT

At the age of 70 George Müller retired and handed over the management of his orphanages to his son-in-law. Müller then went on a series of worldwide missionary tours. From 1875 to 1892 he traveled 250,000 miles and addressed three million people in 42 countries. He died in Bristol, aged 93.

George Müller

✠ FIRST SUNDAY SCHOOLS

The first Sunday Schools were started in England in 1759 by the Methodist Hannah Ball, but it was left to a printer to expand these schools into a Christian education movement. Robert Raikes, an Anglican layman, had been apprenticed to his father, a printer who founded the Gloucester Journal. Raikes took over as editor of the Gloucester Journal when his father died and used it to expose the terrible conditions inside prisons. Raikes came to realize that the prisons were full of people whose lives had been shaped by their deprived childhood, so he focused his attention on the poor, uneducated children who roamed the London streets. He set about organizing the few existing Sunday Schools and is credited with founding the Sunday School movement. His first Sunday School was started in 1766 in Catherine Street, London, for the ragged children who spent their time in 'cursing and swearing and riot.' In 1788 John Wesley wrote to a friend, 'I verily think these Sunday Schools are one of the noblest specimens of charity which have been set on foot in England since William the Conqueror.' In the US, Francis Asbury began the first Sunday School in Virginia in 1786. He based it on Raikes' model and provided simple lessons in reading and spelling, Scripture memorization and the learning of hymns.Today's individual Sunday Schools and organizations like the *World Council of Christian Education* and

George Whitefield (left) and John Wesley (right) two great evangelists from the 18th century.

Scripture Union are the heirs to Raikes' Sunday School movement.

✣ GREATEST JESUIT MISSIONARY

Francis Xavier, 1506-1552, was known as 'the apostle to the Indies and to Japan' for his pioneer missionary work in the East Indies and Japan.

✣ MOST-TRAVELED 18TH-CENTURY MAN

George Whitefield, an Anglican evangelist and friend of John and Charles Wesley, not only traveled throughout Britain preaching the gospel, but he also made seven preaching tours to America between 1738 and 1770. He was the most well-traveled evangelist of his day and always drew large crowds to all his meetings. His second tour, 1739-41, is especially remembered for the widespread revival which broke out at his meetings.

✣ HORSEBACK EVANGELIST

John Wesley used to write in his notebooks and prepare his sermons on horseback. He sometimes traveled over 10,000 miles a year by horse, preaching three or four times a day.

✣ FIRST EVANGELIST TO CALL PEOPLE TO THE FRONT

Charles Finney, 1792-1875, the American evangelist and revivalist preacher, pressed for decisions at his meetings. He was the first to have an 'invitation' calling people to the front to make a public witness of their conversion.

✣ IMPORTANT SECOND FIDDLES

The leaders of the Reformation often had important assistants. Luther had Melanchthon, Zwingli had Bullinger, Calvin had Farel and Tyndale had Frith. 'It takes more grace than I can tell, To play the second fiddle well.'
C. H. SPURGEON

✣ MOST INFLUENTIAL REFORMED THEOLOGIAN

Calvin's understanding of the Bible spread to Scotland, Poland, Holland, and America. His spiritual descendants make up the World Alliance of Reformed Churches based in Calvin's Geneva. This worldwide alliance consists of 178 denominations with over 50 million adherents in more than 80 countries.

REFORMERS OF SOCIETY

It is a mark of the grace of God that so many Christians have been in the forefront of reforming society and caring for the poor, sick, marginalized, and rejected. They attempt to bring Christ's healing and compassion to men and women as they follow in the footsteps of the One who spoke about the need for people to be light and salt in society.

Benwell's sketch of a ward at the hospital at Scutari. In the center Florence Nightingale holds up her lamp. She transformed the wards beyond recognition.

✠ GREATEST ARMY HEALTH REFORM

By the middle of the 19th century more British soldiers died in the barracks than on the battlefield. All this changed after Florence Nightingale, a devout Christian, was put in charge of the military hospitals at Scutari in Turkey, during the Crimean War. When she went to Scutari, Florence was horrified by the living conditions of the soldiers. The total water allowance for all washing and drinking was one pint per person per day. The barracks were filthy and infested with rats and fleas. As a result of her dedicated work and fight against incompetence and indifference the appalling death rate was reduced.

By May 1855 Florence Nightingale had become concerned for the welfare of soldiers throughout the British Empire, but especially in India. With her friend Sidney Herbert, the Secretary of State for War, she resolved to improve the health and living conditions of soldiers throughout the world, with remarkable success.

Also, as a result of her reforming work for nurses, and the enormous respect and admiration in which Florence was held, the status of the nursing profession was raised to new heights. She introduced a uniform for nurses, and founded a nurses' training school at St Thomas' Hospital, London. Nurses were never again regarded and treated as the dregs of society.

✠ LARGEST RESCUE MISSION

Union Rescue Mission is the largest, and one of the oldest, rescue missions in the United States. It provides emergency services, residential recovery programs, and the good news to the poor and homeless of Los Angeles.

JONI EARECKSON TADA

✠ MOST FAMOUS QUADRIPLEGIC CHRISTIAN WOMAN

Joni Eareckson Tada is the founder and president of *JAF Ministries* (JAF), an organization accelerating Christian ministry in the disability community.

A diving accident in 1967 left Joni a quadriplegic in a wheelchair, unable to use her hands. During two years of rehabilitation, she spent long months learning how to paint, holding a brush between her teeth. Today, she is an internationally known mouth artist. Her autobiography, *Joni*, also helped her to become well known. Joni's role as an advocate for disabled persons led to a presidential appointment on the National Council on Disability for three and a half years, during which time the *Americans with Disabilities Act* became law.

✠ WHEELS FOR THE WORLD

Through her work with *JAF Ministries*, she records a five-minute radio program

Joni and her husband, 1998.

Joni and Friends, which is heard daily on over 700 broadcast outlets worldwide, and provides information and encouragement to those with disabilities as well as raising disability awareness.

JAF Ministries also collects, refurbishes and distributes wheelchairs around the world, through one of its organizations called, *Wheels for the World*.

✠ BEDLAM STRANGEST NAME FOR BETHLEHEM

The word *bedlam* is a corruption of the name for Bethlehem. In the 1400s, the hospital of the London monastery of St Mary of Bethlehem became a city-run insane asylum. Bethlehem was often pronounced *bedlam*, and the word came to mean the noise and confusion of an insane asylum.

✠ CARE FOR THE SICK AND DYING OF CALCUTTA

Mother Teresa, 1910-97, born Agnes Gouxha Bejaxhu, the daughter of Albanian peasants, devoted herself with two other nuns to caring for the sick and dying from Calcutta's slums. Mother Teresa's *Missionary Sisters of Charity* is now made up of thousands of nuns who work throughout the world.

✠ OLDEST NETWORK ORGANIZATION TO HELP ALCOHOLICS

Alcoholics Victorious, founded in 1948, is the oldest network of Christian support groups, with meetings around the world.

✠ OLDEST CHRISTIAN GROUP WORKING AMONG YOUNG DRUG ADDICTS

Teen Challenge is the oldest, largest and most successful program of its kind in the world, claiming a 70-86% cure rate. It was established in 1958 by David Wilkerson (of *Cross and the Switchblade* fame). *Teen Challenge* has grown to more than 120 centers in the United States and 250 centers worldwide.

For over 30 years, *Teen Challenge* has been going into schools around the world working with teens to educate them about the dangers of drugs. It also reaches out to people in juvenile halls, jails, and prisons.

INTERNATIONAL UNION OF GOSPEL MISSIONS

✠ CHRISTIAN SOCIAL WORK ON A GRAND SCALE

The *International Union of Gospel Missions* has 272 member ministries, 90% of whom are based in the USA. 242 of these member ministries operate traditional rescue mission programs including overnight shelter, food, etc. In addition to this, they have 21 non-traditional rescue missions, such as rehabilitation programs, community outreach ministries, and Women and Family Ministries.

	Yearly	Daily
Meals Served	27,373,795	74,997
Transient Bed/Nights	5,252,389	14,390
Program Bed/Nights	3,728,156	10,214
Chapel	6,809,462	18,656
Bible Study	1,786,727	4,895
Spiritual Decisions	163,879	449
Counseling Sessions	658,977	1,805
Clothing (number of pieces)	13,670,229	37,453
Program Graduates	12,290	34
PRISON		
Visits	6,430	18
Gospel Services Held	2,919	–
Total Attendance	46,205	127
Spiritual Decisions	3,475	10
CLINICS		
Medical Clinic	143,692	394
Dental Clinic	6,053	17
Eye Clinic	3,972	11
Alcohol Clinic	5,737	16
Detox Center	1,000	3

PRISON WORK

✠ THE OLDEST INTERNATIONAL PRISON MINISTRY

The oldest and most extensive international prison ministry in the world goes by the name of *Worldwide Prison Ministries*. It is headed up by Dr Gene Neill who has held crusades in more than 2,000 prisons, in 44 countries, on five continents. *Worldwide Prison Ministries* has reached hundreds of thousands of inmates for Christ.

Chuck Colson of Prison Ministries International visiting an inmate.

✠ MAN WHO HAS SPOKEN TO THE GREATEST NUMBER OF PRISONERS

Dr Neill has personally been in more prisons and has spoken with more prisoners than any other man in history.

HOSPICE CARE

✠ FIRST HOSPICE

The first 'hospital' for the sole purpose of providing care for the dying was opened in 1967 by Dame Cicely Saunders, in England. St Christopher's Hospice provides pain control and spiritual support for terminally ill cancer patients, allowing them to live lives that are as full and peaceful as possible.

Since 1967 hundreds of hospice units have been opened throughout the world.

✠ EIGHT-YEAR-OLD DENIED CARE

Global enlargement of the hospice movement resulted from an eight-year-old boy being denied hospice support. In 1983, *Children's Hospice International* (CHI) was founded as a non-profit organization to

A children's hospice is not just a place where children die. It is a whole organization dedicated to helping a family.

Leprosy occurs most in the poorest countries.

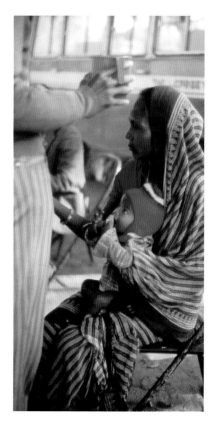

LEPROSY WORK

✤ CARING FOR 'THE WORLD'S LEAST AND LAST'

In 1997, more than 29,000 people were cured of leprosy through the *American Leprosy Missions' Campaign to Cure*. Founded in 1906, *American Leprosy Missions (ALM)* provides care to people around the world with leprosy and disabilities. *ALM* is a non-denominational Christian ministry of hope and restoration for those suffering with the disease. The ministry now supports more than 150 projects in 24 countries.

✤ C. EVERETT KOOP

'If the children receive the cure [from leprosy] in time, they don't have to suffer at all; if they don't receive the cure, their suffering will never end.'
C. EVERETT KOOP US SURGEON GENERAL (RETIRED)

✤ RUTH BELL GRAHAM

'The Bible tells us that Jesus not only healed those with leprosy, he touched them. That, to me, is the most important aspect of the wonderful work done by *American Leprosy Missions*. They don't just heal people with leprosy, they touch them with the love and hope of Jesus. Can we do any less?'
RUTH BELL GRAHAM

✤ JONI

'I care about people with disabilities and that's why I am 100% behind the work of *American Leprosy Missions*. Our friends at *ALM* are laboring among the world's least and last persons with disabilities – giving them help and hope in Christ.'
JONI EARECKSON TADA

provide a network of support and care for children with life-threatening conditions and for their families.

It was in 1977 that an eight-year-old boy was denied hospice support because he was a child. This denial triggered the crusade for children's hospice care and the official development of *CHI*. Initially, only four hospice programs in the United States would accept children. *CHI* has worked effectively to dramatically change these numbers. Today, 447 programs include children as patients and almost all of the existing 2,000 hospice programs will consider accepting a child.

20TH-CENTURY EVANGELISM

To proclaim their message, Christian organizations have harnessed modern methods of communication, from radio, to television, to live satellite link-ups. The Billy Graham Evangelistic Association was a pioneer in this field with production of television programs such as *The Hour of Decision*, and films like *The Hiding Place*. Billy Graham himself has witnessed to many well-known individuals, such as Steve McQueen when he was dying of cancer, as well as having numerous meetings with American Presidents – Truman, Eisenhower, Kennedy, Nixon, Ford, Carter, Reagan and Clinton.

✣ **BIGGEST WORLD RELIGION**
Christianity has the largest number of adherents of all the world faiths. Nearly one in three – 30% of the people in the world – profess some kind of Christian belief.

✣ **NON-CHRISTIAN WORLD**
The rate of increase of those who profess a Christian faith lags behind the rate of increase of non-Christians. By the year 2010 it is predicted that about one in four – 27% of the people in the world – will be Christians.

✣ **SECOND LARGEST RELIGION**
Islam is at present the second largest world religion. But at its present rate of increase it is predicted that there could be more Muslims in the world than Christians by the year 2010.

✣ **'CHRISTIAN' AMERICA**
87% of North Americans identify themselves with Christianity.

Almost one in three people in the world profess some kind of Christian faith.

✣ A 30% CHRISTIAN WORLD

If we could shrink the earth's population to a village of precisely 100 people, with all the existing human ratios remaining the same, it would look like this. There would be:

- 57 Asians
- 21 Europeans
- 14 from the western hemisphere
- 8 Africans
- 52 female
- 48 male
- 70 non-white
- 30 white
- 70 non-Christian
- 30 Christian
- 89 heterosexual
- 11 homosexual/lesbian
- 59% of the entire world's wealth would be in the hands of only 6 people and all 6 would be citizens of the United States
- 80 in substandard housing
- 70 unable to read
- 50 suffering from malnutrition
- 1 with a college education
- 1 owning a computer

✣ CHRISTIANS BY CONTINENT

The greatest number of Christians live in Europe.

Europe
460,000,000
29%

Asia
210,000,000
13%

Oceania
20,000,000
1%

Africa
250,000,000
16%

North America
350,000,000
22%

South America
310,000,000
19%

✠ DENOMINATIONS

Worldwide, there are about:

900,000,000	Roman Catholics	
135,000,000	Orthodox	
95,000,000	Pentecostals	
87,000,000	Lutherans	
66,000,000	Baptists	
53,000,000	Anglicans	
48,000,000	Presbyterians	
27,000,000	Methodists	

✠ LARGEST RELIGIOUS ORGANIZATION

The Roman Catholic Church is the world's largest religious organization. It has nearly 800 archbishops, more than 3,000 bishops, over 400,000 priests and almost 900,000 nuns.

THE MERRITT MINISTRY

✠ MOST UNUSUAL METHOD OF EVANGELISM

Founded in October 1977, *The Merritt Ministry*, according to its mission statement, seeks to 'magnify and exemplify the love of Christ Jesus through visual means (hot and cold air inflatables) as well as through philanthropic and ministry outreaches.'

Currently, *The Merritt Ministry* has two hot air, special shaped balloons. They are *Jesus, the hot air balloon*, which is 100 feet high, and *Arky, the hot air balloon*, which is 85 feet high. These 'gentle giants' draw the attention of large crowds of people, enabling the gospel of Jesus to be shared with them.

✠ NORTH AMERICA'S MOST COMPLEX HOT AIR BALLOON

Arky has a capacity of 131,000 cubic feet of air, about twice that of an average hot air balloon, with over 1,700 individual patterns. It is the conception of Rev and Mrs Rohn Peterson and the children of the battered children's home where Rev Peterson is an administrator. *Arky* has been used as a vehicle to draw attention to the plight of abused children.

LEAST EVANGELIZED

The least evangelized people of the world are the concern of the *AD2000 & Beyond Movement*. Their goal was 'a church for every people by the year 2000.' To achieve this they aimed to establish 'a pioneer church planting movement within every country of the world by December 31, 2000.'

✠ ASIA AND PARTS OF NORTH AFRICA

AD2000 & Beyond Movement drew up a list in 1995 which identified the least evangelized people in the world. The list contained 2,500 people groups with more than 10,000 in each group. The greatest number were found in Asia and parts of North Africa.

PROFILE OF THE 20TH CENTURY'S BEST-KNOWN EVANGELIST – BILLY GRAHAM

✠ GRAHAM'S FAMILY

William Franklin Graham, Jr, known as Billy Graham to most of the world, was born on November 7, 1918, near Charlotte, North Carolina, to William Franklin and Morrow Coffey Graham. In 1934, Billy attended a series of revival meetings led by evangelist Mordecai Fowler Ham. Ham's preaching, which heightened Graham's conviction of his sin, led Graham to commit his life to Christ.

✠ COLLEGE

In the fall of 1936, Billy began attending the fundamentalist school, Bob Jones College, in Cleveland, Tennessee. In January of 1937 he transferred to Florida Bible Institute from which he graduated in 1940 with a BTh (Bachelor of Theology degree). While at FBI, he was baptized at a Baptist church and began his life-long membership in the Southern Baptist Convention. Graham attended Wheaton College from 1940 to 1943, when he graduated with a BA in anthropology.

✠ RUTH BELL

At Wheaton, Billy met fellow student Ruth Bell, his future wife. She was the daughter of the Southern Presbyterian surgeon and missionary to China, L. Nelson Bell. Ruth and Billy married on August 13, 1943, after graduation.

✠ YOUTH FOR CHRIST

Graham's first (and only) pastorate was at the Baptist church in the Chicago suburb of Western Springs where he served a little over a year. Graham left that church to become vice president of *Youth for Christ*. For the next four years, he traveled all over the United States, Canada, and Europe speaking at rallies and organizing *YFC* chapters. Gradually, as Graham began to hold evangelistic rallies on his own, his work for *YFC* tapered off, and in 1948 he resigned from the staff.

✠ EVANGELISTIC CAMPAIGNS

Usually working with Billy were soloist George Beverly Shea; choir director and master of ceremonies, Cliff Barrows (whom he met in 1945); and associate evangelist Grady Wilson. Graham was quite well known within evangelical and fundamentalist communities in America, but at the end of 1949, he suddenly came into national prominence when the newspaper magnate, William Randolph Hearst, for reasons unknown, ordered his publications to 'puff Graham' and other newspapers around the country followed suit. His campaign in Los Angeles, planned for three weeks, lasted seven.

In the next decade, Billy Graham held evangelistic campaigns in all the major US cities as well as rallies in Africa, Asia, South America, and Europe. Perhaps the most impressive meetings of his career were the Greater London Crusade of 1954 and the New York Crusade of 1957. After 1957 Graham generally held three to five crusades a year.

✠ BGEA

The *Billy Graham Evangelistic Association* (*BGEA*), which had been formed in 1954, was one of, if not the, major influence on five major 20th-century evangelical events: the founding of *Christianity Today* magazine in 1955, the *World Congress on Evangelism* in Berlin in 1966, the *International Congress on World Evangelization* in Lausanne in 1974, and the 1983 and 1986 *International Conferences of Itinerant Evangelists*.

Billy Graham
at Earls Court,
London.

✜ WHO WILL TAKE OVER FROM BILLY?

In 1992 it was announced by the *BGEA* that Graham had Parkinson's disease and so would not be able to do so much work. In 1996, Graham's eldest son, William Franklin Graham III, was made vice chairman of the *BGEA* board and it was announced he would be his father's successor when the time came for Billy Graham to leave the ministry.

✜ PREACHED TO THE MOST PEOPLE

Evangelist Billy Graham has preached the gospel to more people in live audiences than anyone else. He has spoken to over 210 million people in more than 185 countries and territories.

✜ BROADCASTING TO OVER 900 RADIO STATIONS

The *BGEA* broadcasts the weekly *Hour of Decision* radio program to more than 900 stations around the world.

✜ MOST 'DOMINANT' FIGURE

Billy Graham is regularly listed by the Gallup organization as one of the 'Ten Most Admired Men in the World' and was described by them as the dominant figure in that poll over the past 45 years. He made an unparalleled 39 appearances, 32 of which were consecutive.

Part 3

CHRISTIAN THOUGHT

3.1
WRITERS AND
WRITINGS

3.2
MOTTOES
AND SAYINGS

3.3
CHRISTIANITY
AND SCIENCE

3.4
A VARIETY OF
VIEWS

3.1 WRITERS AND WRITINGS

Christianity is a written religion and throughout its history, writing has played an important part in spreading 'the word' and in deepening faith. When Johann Gutenberg pioneered movable metal type at Mainz in Germany in 1445, little did he imagine the global revolution in communication his invention would produce. The invention of printing has even been called Germany's greatest contribution to the Renaissance. For Christianity, it meant that Bibles could now be printed in volume, and so bring about in an unimaginable way the dream of the 15th-century scholar Erasmus: 'I wish that the Scriptures might be translated into all languages, so that not only the Scots and the Irish, but also the Turk and the Saracen might read and understand them. I long that the farm-laborer might sing them as he follows his plow, the weaver hum them to the tune of his shuttle, the traveler beguile the weariness of his journey with their stories.'

✧ FIRST CHRISTIAN WRITING AFTER THE BIBLE

At the end of the first century, Clement of Rome, a disciple of Peter and Paul, wrote a letter to the church at Corinth. This is probably the earliest Christian document we have outside of the New Testament.

✧ FIRST DIARY OF A CHRISTIAN WOMAN

The diary of Perpetua was written in c. AD 202 from prison. In it she wrote: 'The dungeon became to me as it were a palace.' Perpetua, age 22, came from Carthage in North Africa and had recently had a baby boy. She was put in prison for her Christian faith, and her diary is the first document we know of from the pen of a Christian woman.

✧ FIRST BOOK TO BE WRITTEN IN ENGLISH BY A WOMAN

The English anchoress Julian of Norwich's *Revelations of Divine Love* is the first book written in the English language by a woman.

✧ INFLUENTIAL MISSIONARY DIARY

David Brainerd, 1718-47, died aged 29. He spent his life ministering to Indians and became one of America's most influential missionaries. After Brainerd's death, Jonathan Edwards edited and published his diary. This diary had a great influence on many future generations of Christian missionaries, including missionaries such as William Carey, Henry Martyn, and Jim Elliot.

✠ AN UNUSUAL GIFT FROM A DEAN OF ST PAUL'S CATHEDRAL

'The Cross, my seal in baptism, spread below
Doth by that form into an anchor grow.
Crosses grow anchors, bear as thou should'st do
Thy cross, and that cross grows an anchor too.
But he that makes our crosses anchors thus
Is Christ, Who there is crucified for us.'
JOHN DONNE C. 1572-1631 THE FAMOUS ENGLISH POET AND PREACHER, DEAN OF ST PAUL'S CATHEDRAL, LONDON

John Donne wrote these words to go with a signet ring that he gave to Izaak Walton. On the ring was an engraving of Christ crucified with the cross in the shape of an anchor.

PRISON WRITINGS

✠ PAUL'S PRISON LETTERS

The apostle Paul wrote the largest number of letters in the New Testament. Of the 13 he wrote, Ephesians, Philippians, Colossians, and Philemon are called his 'prison' letters. In addition to those four, 2 Timothy was also written while Paul was in prison, or under house arrest.

✠ *PILGRIM'S PROGRESS*

John Bunyan, 1628-88 wrote the first part of *The Pilgrim's Progress* during the time he was in Bedford jail. Convicted under an old statute of Elizabeth I, which provided that any person who should frequent conventicals (non-conformist religious meetings – Bunyan was a Puritan) or persuade others to, should be committed to prison, and remain there till he should conform. It was therefore imprisonment for an indefinite

John Bunyan. From the frontispiece of *The Pilgrim's Progress*.

period. He spent much of the period between 1660-72 in prison, and was again imprisoned for six months around 1678.

✠ DIETRICH BONHOEFFER

One of Dietrich Bonhoeffer's books is called *Letters and Papers from Prison*. It reflects his Christian thinking in his prison cell as he awaited trial for plotting to assassinate Hitler. Bonhoeffer wrote, 'When Christ calls a man he bids him come and die.'

✠ ALEXANDER SOLZHENITSYN

Solzhenitsyn, who was imprisoned from 1945-53, exposed the evil system of prison camps inside the former Soviet Union in which millions of prisoners died. *Gulag* is an acronym in Russian of the name meaning Chief Administration of Corrective Labor Camps.

✠ MARTIN LUTHER KING

King, frequently imprisoned for leading the Civil Rights movement in USA, often used this time to write important documents and protests.

Martin Luther King.

✣ CHRISTIANS IN ANTWERP

In 1568 Scobland, Hues and Coomans, three leading Protestant Christians who lived in the capital city of the Netherlands during a time of vicious persecution, were arrested in Antwerp. Scobland and Coomans were burned alive and Hues died in prison. In a letter from prison they wrote:

'Since it is the will of the Almighty that we should suffer for his name, we patiently submit; though the flesh may rebel against the spirit, yet the truths of the gospel shall support us, and Christ shall bruise the serpent's head.

'We are comforted, for we have faith; we fear not affliction, for we have hope; we forgive our enemies, for we have charity.

Do not worry about us, we are happy because of God's promises and exult in being thought worthy to suffer for Christ's sake.

We do not desire release, but fortitude; we ask not for liberty, but for the power of perseverance;

we wish for no change but that which places a crown of victory on our heads.'

GREGORY THE GREAT

✣ THE SEVEN DEADLY SINS

The table below lists the seven deadly sins (vices) in the traditional order, with the virtues against which they are sins. This list can be dated back to the time of Pope Gregory the Great, but the Bible proscribes them all.

VICE	VIRTUE AGAINST WHICH IT SINS
Pride	Humility
Avarice/Greed	Generosity
Envy	Love
Wrath/Anger	Kindness
Lust	Self control
Gluttony	Faith and temperance
Sloth	Zeal

BOOKS THAT CHANGED PEOPLE

✣ RULES AND EXERCISES OF HOLY LIVING AND DYING

John Wesley's deep concern for the interior life and the spiritual pilgrimage of the Christian was set alight when he read Bishop Jeremy Taylor's *Holy Living and Holy Dying.* 'God hath given to man a short time here upon earth, and yet upon this short time eternity depends.'

'Christianity has had its most glorious effect on your heart when it has changed your spirit, removed all the pride of life from you, and made you delight in humbling yourselves beneath the lowest of all your fellow-creatures.'
JEREMY TAYLOR

Martin Luther.

✣ LUTHER'S COMMENTARY ON THE LETTER TO THE GALATIANS

In his commentary on Paul's letter to the Galatians, Martin Luther expounds Paul's teaching on the grace, power, glory, and security of the life of faith in Jesus Christ. He shows that this is the truth which seekers for peace with God need to hear.

John Bunyan prized Luther's commentary on Galatians. Bunyan wrote: 'The God in whose hands are all our days and ways, did cast into my hand, one day, a book of Martin Luther; it was his comment on the Galatians which, when I had but a little way perused, I found my condition, in his experience, so largely and profoundly handled, as if his book had been written out of my own heart. I do prefer this book of Martin Luther on the Galatians, excepting the Holy Bible, before all books that ever I have seen, as most fit for a wounded conscience.'

Luther's commentary on Galatians also acted as midwife in the conversion of Charles Wesley, the 'Sweet singer of Methodism.' On May 17, 1738, Charles Wesley wrote in his Journal for that day, 'I spent some hours this evening in private with Martin Luther, who was greatly blessed to me, especially the conclusion of the second chapter of Galatians. I labored, waited and prayed to feel "who loved me, and gave himself for me,"' On May 21, four days later, assured faith dawned in Charles Wesley's heart.

Commenting on the last phrase of Galatians chapter 2, verse 20, Martin Luther wrote: '"Who loved me and gave himself for me." Here Paul shows us the true way of justification and a perfect example of the assurance of faith. Anyone who can with a firm and constant faith say with Paul, "I live by faith in the Son of God, who loved me and gave himself for me" is happy indeed. With those words Paul takes away the whole righteousness of the law and works. We must therefore carefully consider these last words. It was not I who first loved the Son of God and gave myself for him. Wicked people who are puffed up with the wisdom of the flesh imagine they

The Templeton Prize, an award to encourage progress in religion, is the largest annual prize awarded in the world. It is worth over one million dollars. It was established in 1972 by Sir John Templeton, a Tennessee-born financial analyst and Presbyterian layman, and first presented in 1973. Most of the winners of the Templeton Foundation Prize have written influential Christian books.

Winners

1973	Mother Teresa of Calcutta, founder of the Missionaries of Charity
1974	Brother Roger, Founder and Prior of the Taize Community in France
1975	Dr Sarvepalli Radhakrishnan, former President of India and Oxford Professor of Eastern Religions and Ethics
1976	HE Leon Joseph Cardinal Suenens, Archbishop of Malines-Brussels
1978	Prof Thomas F Torrance, President of International Academy of Religion and Sciences, Scotland
1981	Dame Cicely Saunders, Originator of Modern Hospice Movement, England
1982	The Rev Dr Billy Graham, Founder, The Billy Graham Evangelistic Association
1983	Alexander Solzhenitsyn, USA
1984	The Rev Michael Bourdeaux, Founder of Keston College, England
1989	The Very Rev Lord MacLeod of the Iona Community, Scotland
1991	The Rt Hon Lord Jakobovits, Chief Rabbi of Great Britain and the Commonwealth
1992	Dr Kyung-Chik Han, founder of Seoul's Young Nak Presbyterian Church
1993	Charles W Colson, Founder, Prison Fellowship, Virginia
1994	Michael Novak, Scholar at the American Enterprise Institute, Washington, DC
1996	William R 'Bill' Bright, founder of Campus Crusade for Christ.
1998	Sir Sigmund Sternberg, founder of London's Sternberg Center for Judaism.

do what they can—they love God, they give themselves for Christ; but what they are doing is abolishing the Gospel and deriding Christ. They say he is a justifier and a Savior, but in fact they take from him the power both to justify and to save, and they give it to their own actions, ceremonies, and devotions. This is to live in their own righteousness and actions, and not by faith in the Son of God.'

✠ THE RISE AND PROGRESS OF RELIGION IN THE SOUL

At the age of 26, William Wilberforce read Philip Doddridge's *Rise and Progress of Religion in the Soul* and realized that he was not a Christian. This book helped him to give his life to Christ.

✠ ALL-TIME BEST-SELLING BOOK, AFTER THE BIBLE

After the Bible, John Bunyan's *Pilgrim's Progress* is the world's most widely circulated book. By 1885 it had been published in 74 languages and dialects. The four Chinese editions included a Wenli edition, a Mandarin edition, a Canton Vernacular edition and an Amoy dialect edition.

BILLY GRAHAM'S BOOKS AND PUBLICATIONS

✠ MY ANSWER

His newspaper column, *My Answer*, is carried by newspapers across America and has a combined circulation of more than five million readers.

✠ DECISION

Decision magazine, the official publication of the Billy Graham Evangelistic Association, has a circulation of 1.7 million in 160 countries, making it one of the largest religious periodicals in the world.

✠ EVERY BOOK A TOP SELLER

Billy Graham has written 18 books. Each book became a top seller. His book, *Approaching Hoofbeats: The Four Horsemen of the Apocalypse*, 1983, was listed for several weeks on *The New York Times* best-seller list.

✠ ANGELS

His book, *Angels: God's Secret Agents*, 1975, sold one million copies within 90 days. His book, *The Jesus Generation*, 1971, sold 200,000 copies in the first two weeks.

✠ JUST AS I AM

His most recently published book, his autobiography, *Just As I Am*, published in 1997, achieved a 'triple crown,' appearing simultaneously on the three top best-seller lists in one week.

✠ LARGEST FIRST PRINTING IN HISTORY

Billy Graham's book *How To Be Born Again*, 1977, had the then largest first printing in publishing history with 800,000 copies printed.

TEN FAMOUS CHRISTIAN CLASSICS

- *The Confessions of St Augustine*
- *The Imitation of Christ* by Thomas à Kempis
- *The Practice of the Presence of God* by Brother Lawrence
- *The Twelve Steps of Humility and Pride* by Bernard of Clairvanx
- *A Serious Call to a Devout and Holy Life* by William Law
- *Pensées* by Blaise Pascal
- *The Saints' Everlasting Rest* by Richard Baxter
- *A Treatise Concerning Religious Affections* by Jonathan Edwards
- *The Pilgrim's Progress* by John Bunyan
- *The Book of Martyrs* by John Foxe

MOTTOES AND SAYINGS

Many of the mottoes of famous Christian and philanthropic organizations started off as short pithy sayings which summarized their work. The largest children's charity in the UK today, Dr Barnardo Homes, provides advice and help for over 50,000 homeless, abused or poor children. In 1870 the young Thomas John Barnardo had recently arrived from Dublin to train in London's East End as a doctor. He thought that God might be calling him to be a medical missionary in China until one day he was introduced to the destitute children of London. After seeing their plight, while still a student, he set up the *East End Mission* for destitute children in Stepney. To remind everyone of the aim of this work its motto became, 'No absolutely destitute child ever refused admission.'

Corrie ten Boom.

QUOTES FROM 20TH-CENTURY CHRISTIANS

✠ **CHARLES W. COLSON**
(Served a prison sentence for his involvement in the Watergate cover-up.)
'The Great Commission is far more than evangelism. I think many evangelicals have a very simplistic view of what it is that God is calling us to do. The Great Commission is to make disciples, "teaching them all I have taught you"' (Matthew 28:20).

✠ **JIM ELLIOT**
(Missionary to the Auca Indians.)
'I care not if I never raise my voice again for Him, if only I may love Him, please Him. Maybe in His mercy He shall give me a host of children that I may lead them through the vast star fields to explore His delicacies whose finger ends set them to burning. But if not, if only I may see Him, touch His garments, smile into His eyes – ah then, not stars nor children shall matter, only Himself.'

✠ **JONI EARECKSON TADA**
(Confined to a wheelchair since her diving accident as a teenager.)
'God doesn't just give us grace, He gives us Jesus, the Lord of grace.'

✠ **CORRIE TEN BOOM**
(Put in a Nazi camp for sheltering Jews.)
'Faith sees the invisible, believes the unbelievable, and receives the impossible.'

✠ **JONATHAN EDWARDS**
(Triple-jump world-record-holder.)
'We cannot please God simply by trying hard; we need to be transformed from the inside, and this will only happen if we give God the opportunity.'

✠ MOTHER TERESA OF CALCUTTA
(Founder of the Missionaries of Charity.)
'Giving wholehearted and free service to the poorest of the poor.'

✠ MARTIN LUTHER KING, JR.
'Darkness cannot drive out darkness; only light can do that. Hate cannot drive out hate; only love can do that.'

✠ LUIS PALAU
(Evangelist.)
'Back to the Bible or back to the jungle.'

✠ KENNETH TAYLOR
(Translator of *The Living Bible*.)
'Read the Bible together as a family every day.'

MOST FAMOUS CHRISTIAN QUOTES

✠ AUGUSTINE OF HIPPO
'Our hearts are restless until they find their rest in thee.'

✠ WILLIAM BOOTH
'Go for souls, and go for the worst.'

✠ WILLIAM CAREY
'Expect great things from God. Attempt great things for God.'

✠ BILLY GRAHAM
'My one purpose in life is to help people find a personal relationship with God, which, I believe, comes through knowing Christ.'

✠ TOYOHIKO KAGAWA
'O God, make me like Jesus Christ.'

✠ DAVID LIVINGSTONE
'I will go anywhere provided it is forward.'

✠ HENRY MARTYN
'Let me burn out for God.'

✠ ROBERT MORRISON
'Send me where workers are most needed and difficulties greatest.'

✠ J.H. NEWMAN
'Heart speaks to heart.'

✠ LORD SHAFTESBURY
'The first principle, God's honor; the second, man's happiness; the means, prayer and unremitting diligence.'

✠ MARTIN LUTHER
'Here stand I. I can do no other.'

✠ D. L. MOODY
'I look upon this world as a wrecked vessel. God has given me a lifeboat and said to me, "Moody, save all you can."'

'It is not our strength we want. It is not our work to make them believe. That is the work of the Spirit. Our work is to give them the Word of God. I cannot convert men; I can only proclaim the Gospel.'

✠ HUDSON TAYLOR
'Depend upon it. God's work, done in God's way, will never lack God's supplies.'

✠ TERTULLIAN
'The blood of the martyrs is the seed of the church.'

✠ SMITH WIGGLESWORTH
'Only believe!'

✠ COUNT LUDWIG VON ZINZENDORF
'I have one passion; it is he and he alone.'

David Livingstone.

STATEMENTS OF FAITH OF ORGANIZATIONS AND MOVEMENTS

✠ THE WATCHWORD OF THE REFORMATION

Sola fidi, sola gratis, sola Scriptura
'By faith alone, through grace alone, by the Scriptures alone.'

✠ MISSION OF THE GIDEONS INTERNATIONAL

'That all the people of the earth may know ...' (1 Kings 8:60)

✠ STUDENT VOLUNTEER MOVEMENT

'Evangelization of the world in this generation.'

19th century London – the desperately poor wait outside a fishmonger and poulterer for scraps after the close of business.

✠ DR BARNARDO'S HOMES

'No absolutely destitute child ever refused admission.'

✠ SOCIETY OF JESUS

'To the greater glory of God.'

LAST WORDS

✠ SEVEN LAST SAYINGS OF JESUS

1. 'Father, forgive them; for they know not what they do' (Luke 23:34 *KJV*).
2. 'Today shalt thou be with me in paradise' (Luke 23:43 *KJV*).
3. 'Woman, behold thy son!' (John 19:26 *KJV*).
4. 'My God, my God, why hast thou forsaken me?' (Mark 15:34 *KJV*).
5. 'I thirst' (John 19:28).
6. 'It is finished' (John 19:30).
7. 'Father, into thy hands I commend my spirit' (Luke 23:46 *KJV*).

✠ DAVID

'These are the last words of David:
'When one rules over men in
    righteousness,
  when he rules in the fear of God,
he is like the light of morning at sunrise
    on a cloudless morning,
like the brightness after rain
    that brings the grass from the earth.
... But evil men are all to be cast aside like
    thorns,
  which are not gathered with the hand.
Whoever touches thorns
  uses a tool of iron or the shaft of a spear;
they are burned up where they lie.'
(2 Samuel 23:1, 3-4, 6-7, *NIV*)

✠ JOSEPH ADDISON

'See in what peace a Christian can die.'

✠ RICHARD BAXTER

'I have pain (there is no arguing against sense); but I have peace, I have peace.'

✠ THOMAS À BECKET, ARCHBISHOP OF CANTERBURY

'I am ready to die for my Lord, that in my blood the Church may obtain liberty and peace.'

✠ BERNARD OF CLAIRVAUX

'I beg you, dearest brethren, love one another.'

✠ WILLIAM BOOTH

'While women weep, as they do now, I'll fight; while men go to prison, in and out, in and out, as they do now, I'll fight; where there is a drunkard left, while there is a poor lost girl upon the streets, where there remains one dark soul without the light of God – I'll fight! I'll fight to the very end.'
(End of Booth's last speech.)

✠ DAVID BRAINERD

'I was a little better than speechless all day. O my God, I am speedily coming to thee! Hasten the day, O Lord, if it be thy blessed will. Oh, come, Lord Jesus, come quickly.'

JOSEPH BUTLER

'Though I have endeavored to avoid sin, and to please God to the utmost of my power, yet, from the consciousness of perpetual infirmities, I am still afraid to die. (His chaplain replied: "My Lord, you have forgotten that Jesus Christ is a Savior.") True, but how shall I know that he is a savior for me? ("My Lord," answered the chaplain, "it is written, 'Him that cometh to me I will in no wise cast out.'") True, and I am surprised that, although I have read that Scripture a thousand times over, I have never felt its virtue till this moment; and now I die happy.'

JOHN CALVIN

'Thou, Lord, bruisest me, but I am abundantly satisfied, since it is from thy hand.'

EDWARD THE CONFESSOR

'Weep not, I shall not die; and as I leave the land of the dying I trust to see the blessings of the Lord in the land of the living.'

MATTHEW HENRY

'You have been used to take notice of the sayings of dying men. This is mine: that a life spent in the service of God, and communion with him, is the most comfortable and pleasant life that anyone can live in this world.'

John Knox.

JOHN KNOX

'Live in Christ, live in Christ, and the flesh need not fear death.'

THOMAS LINCOLN

(Father of Abraham Lincoln.) 'Abe, I'm going to leave you now and I shall not return. I want you to be kind to your mother and live as I have taught you. Love your heavenly Father and keep his commandments.'

MARTIN LUTHER

'God so loved the world that he gave his only begotten Son, that whosoever believeth in him should not perish but have everlasting life.' (Repeated three times.)

D.L. Moody preached to large crowds in many countries.

ROBERT MURRAY M'CHEYNE

(As he lay dying, aged 29) 'God gave me a message to deliver and a horse to ride. Alas, I have killed the horse and now I cannot deliver the message.'

F. B. MEYER

'You will tell the others I am going home a little sooner than I thought. Then tell them not to talk about the servant but to talk about the Savior.'

D.L. MOODY

'Earth is receding; heaven is approaching. This is my crowning day!'

WALTER RALEIGH

'Even such is time which takes in trust
Our youth, our joys, and all we have
And pays us but with age and dust:
Who in the dark and silent grave
When we have wandered all our ways
Shuts up the glory of our days.
And from the earth and grave and dust
The Lord shall raise me up, I trust.'
(Written on the day before he was beheaded.)

HUDSON TAYLOR

'I am so weak that I can hardly write, I cannot read my Bible, I cannot even pray, I can only lie still in God's arms like a little child, and trust.'

JOHN WESLEY

'The best of all is, God is with us. Farewell!'

Hudson Taylor, founder of the China Inland Mission.

.3 CHRISTIANITY AND SCIENCE

Christians have had a strong and distinctive influence on scientific thinking over the centuries. Francis Bacon (1561-1626), English philosopher and essayist, saw in Scripture a clear mandate for altering the natural world for the benefit of humankind.

Many scientists have viewed scientific research as bringing more glory to God. Thus John Kepler (1571-1630), in studying the heavens which declare the glory of God, stated that he was merely 'thinking God's thoughts after him.' This became a powerful motive for the scientific exploration of nature. In recent years, an increasing number of scientists are coming to believe that the complexity and mathematical precision of the universe can only be explained by the existence of a Creator God.

SCIENTISTS AND THEIR CHRISTIAN FAITH

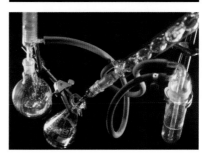

The number of scientists who have made no secret of their Christian faith is impressive. Some are listed here.

- **Sir Isaac Newton**: 'There is but one God the Father of whom are all things and we in him and one Lord Jesus Christ by whom are all things and we by him.'

  'No sciences are better attested than the religion of the Bible.'

- **Paul Davies**, Australian cosmologist, head of theoretical physics at University of Adelaide: 'It is hard to resist the impression that the present structure of the universe, apparently so sensitive to minor alterations in numbers, has been rather carefully thought out.'

- **Michael Faraday**: 'Since peace is alone in the gift of God; and as it is He who gives it, why should we be afraid? His unspeakable gift in His beloved Son is the ground of no doubtful hope. (*Letter written to a fellow scientist.*)

  'Speculations I have none. I'm resting on certainties. "For I know whom I have believed, and am persuaded that he is able to keep that which I have committed unto him against that day."' (*Nearing death, quoting from 2 Timothy 1:12 KJV.*)

Michael Faraday.

- **Nicolas Copernicus**, astronomer: 'I regard my research as a loving duty to seek the truth in all things, in so far as God has granted.'

Johannes Kepler: 'There are two big books, the book of nature and the book of supernature, the Bible.'

Blaise Pascal: 'The evidence of God's existence and his gift is more than compelling, but those who insist that they have no need of him or it will always find ways to discount the offer.'

Robert Boyle: 'We must not expect to be able to resolve all difficulties, and answer all objections, since we can never directly answer those which require for their solution a perfect comprehension of what is infinite.'

Louis Pasteur, discoverer of the medical use of penicillin: 'The more I study nature, the more I am amazed at the Creator.'

Galileo Galilei: 'I do not feel obliged to believe that the same God who has endowed us with sense, reason, and

Center:
Albert Einstein.

Louis Pasteur.

intellect has intended us to forgo their use.

'Since the Holy Spirit did not intend to teach us whether heaven moves or stands still, nor whether the earth is located at its center or off to one side, then so much the less was it intended to settle for us any other conclusion of the same kind.

'Now if the Holy Spirit has purposely neglected to teach us propositions of this sort as irrelevant to the highest goal (that is, to our salvation), how can anyone affirm that it is obligatory to take sides on them?

'I would say here something that was heard from an ecclesiastic of the most eminent degree: "The intention of the Holy Spirit is to teach us how one goes to heaven, not how heaven goes."'

Albert Einstein: 'It has become appallingly obvious that our technology has exceeded our humanity.'

Robert Jastrow, founder and director of the Institute for Space Studies at the Goddard Space Flight Center, writes frequently about science's confirmation of theism.

Arthur L Schawlow is Professor of Physics at Stanford University and shared the 1981 Physics Nobel Prize with Bloembergen and Siegbahn for their contribution to the development of laser spectroscopy. Schawlow says: 'It seems to me that when confronted with the marvels of life and the universe, one must ask why and not just how. The only possible answers are religious … I find a need for God in the universe and in my own life.'

Henry 'Fritz' Schaefer is the Graham Perdue Professor of Chemistry and director of the Center for Computational Quantum Chemistry at the University of Georgia. He is a five-time nominee for the Nobel Prize and was recently cited as the third most quoted chemist in the world. In a US *News & World Report* article on creation, he wrote: 'My goal is to understand a little corner of God's plan.'

SPACE RESEARCH AND CHRISTIANITY

Wernher von Braun, chief rocket engineer for the German V2 program in World War II. In the 1960s he was director of the Marshall Space Flight Center and an administrator for planning at NASA headquarters until 1972: 'In this modern world of ours many people seem to think that science has somehow made such religious ideas as immortality

untimely or old fashioned. I think science has a real surprise for the skeptics. Science, for instance, tells us that nothing in nature, not even the tiniest particle, can disappear without a trace. Nature does not know extinction. All it knows is transformation. If God applies this fundamental principle to the most minute and insignificant parts of His universe, doesn't it make sense to assume that He applies it to the masterpiece of His creation, the human soul?'

L. Gordon Cooper, Jr: 'Father, we thank you, especially for letting me fly this flight ... for the privilege of being able to be in this position, to be in this wondrous place, seeing all these many startling, wonderful things that you have created.' (*Prayer while orbiting the earth in a space capsule.*)

Jack Lousma, astronaut: 'If I can't believe that the spacecraft I fly assembled itself, how can I believe that the universe assembled itself? I'm convinced only an intelligent God could have built a universe like this.'

Frank Borman: 'I did not see him either, ... but I saw his evidence.' (*Reply to a journalist, on his return flight around the moon with Apollo 8, against the background of a Soviet cosmonaut who said that he had not seen any angels or God in space.*)

GALILEO

✣ THE CRIME OF GALILEO

The indictment of 1630:

'Whereas you, Galileo, son of the late Vincenzio Galilei, of Florence, aged 70 years, were denounced in 1615, by this Holy Office, for holding as true a false doctrine taught by many, namely, that the sun is immovable in the center of the world, and that the earth moves ... therefore this Holy Tribunal states: "The proposition that the sun is in the center of the world and immovable from its place is absurd, philosophically false, and formally heretical; because it is expressly contrary to Holy Scriptures.

'"The proposition that the earth is not the center of the world, nor immovable, but that it moves, and also with a diurnal action, is also absurd, philosophically false, and, theologically considered, at least erroneous in faith."

'Therefore ... invoking the most holy name of our Lord Jesus Christ and of His Most Glorious Mother Mary, We pronounce this Our final sentence: We pronounce, judge, and declare, that you, the said Galileo ... have rendered yourself vehemently suspected by this Holy Office of heresy. ... From which it is Our pleasure that you be absolved, provided that with a sincere heart and unfeigned faith, in Our presence, you abjure, curse, and detest, the said error and heresies, and every other error and heresy contrary to the Catholic and Apostolic Church of Rome.'

✣ A RARE PAPAL APOLOGY

In 1992 Pope John Paul II finally admitted that the Roman Catholic Church had been wrong 349 years earlier to condemn and silence Galileo for saying that the earth moved around the sun.

Pope John Paul II also apologized for the St Bartholomew's Day Massacre in the 16th century when 5,000 Protestants were killed in France.

✣ QUOTE FROM AN ASTRONOMER

'I am inclined to think that the authority of Holy Scripture is intended to convince men of those truths which are necessary for their salvation, which, being far above man's understanding, can not be made credible by any learning, or any other means than revelation by the Holy Spirit.'
GALILEO GALILEI

PASCAL

✣ CHRISTIAN COMPUTER LANGUAGE?

Blaise Pascal (1623-1662), the French scientific genius was also a devout Christian, and he had a computer language named after him, 'Pascal,' in recognition of his first mechanical calculator, which he constructed when he was 19 years old.

Pascal wrote: 'The heart has its reasons that reason does not know ... What a vast distance there is between knowing God and loving him ... Human things must be known to be loved: but Divine things must be loved to be known.'

FARADAY

✣ MOST FAMOUS SANDEMANIAN

Michael Faraday was recognized as the greatest scientist of his own day. He worked at the Royal Institute in London for 50 years and became a leading chemist, discovering benzene. He was also the first to convert mechanical energy into electric energy. He belonged to a group of Christians known as the Sandemanians who interpreted the Bible in a literal way and tried to model themselves on the pattern of the New Testament church.

In 1861 Faraday wrote to a fellow scientist: 'Since peace is alone in the gift of God; and as it is He who gives it, why should we be afraid? His unspeakable gift in His beloved Son is the ground of no doubtful hope.'

CHRISTIANS AND EVOLUTION

Many top scientists, like Michael Faraday, still believe that any form of evolution goes against the teaching of the Bible and that the best way to interpret the first three chapters of the Bible is in a literalistic way.

✣ VIEWPOINT OF A PRO-EVOLUTION SCIENTIST

There are, however, some Bible-believing geneticists who are reverently agnostic about exactly how the accounts of creation in Genesis should be understood:

'If humankind being made "in God's image" is taken to mean qualities God gave to a chosen animal at a particular time in history, then [for the Christian] there is no difficulty about accepting the conventional scientific view of human evolution. The Christian believes that his ancestors subsequently fell from fellowship with God, but this is outside the scope of the scientist, either to confirm or deny. On the other hand if, as some Christians hold, the idea of "God's image" requires that God created the human body and soul together in a separate act, then clearly the Christian must part company with any theory that we have genetic continuity with other animals.' PROFESSOR R.J. BERRY (*The Lion Handbook of Christian Belief*, p. 211.)

✣ VIEWPOINT OF A PRO-EVOLUTION THEOLOGIAN

'I cannot see that at least some forms of the theory of evolution contradict or are contradicted by the Genesis revelation. Scripture reveals religious truths about God, that his creative program culminated in man; science suggests that "evolution" may have been the mode which God employed in creating.

'I recognize, however, that other Christians who accept and uphold the authority of Scripture reject the theory of evolution as being (in their view) incompatible with biblical teaching. As the debate continues, it is particularly important for all of us (whichever position we hold) to try to distinguish both between scientific fact and scientific theory, and distinguish between what the Bible plainly asserts and what we may like to think it asserts.'
JOHN STOTT

✣ WAS ADAM THE FIRST MAN?

'I myself believe in the historicity of Adam and Eve, as the original couple from whom the human race is descended. But my acceptance of Adam and Eve as historical is not incompatible with my belief that several forms of pre-Adamic 'hominid' may have existed for thousands of years previously. They made their cave drawings and buried their dead. It is conceivable that God created Adam out of one of them. You may call them homo erectus. I think you may even call some of them homo sapiens, for these are arbitrary scientific names. But Adam was the first homo divinus, if I may coin the phrase, the first man to whom may be given the biblical designation 'made in the image of God'.
JOHN STOTT (*Understanding the Bible*, p. 63.)

✣ MIRACLES

A miracle 'explained' does not mean that Christians exercise any less faith in God. To the question, 'Is a virgin conception possible?' Christian geneticists come up with different answers.

Parthenogenesis, the technical name for virgin birth, occurs naturally in greenfly and bees. Unfertilized rabbits' eggs have been submitted to chemical and physical shocks and embryos are the result. It has been claimed that parthenogenetic rabbits exist.

The key question is: 'What about the Y-chromosome?' For a human to be born like this the baby would need the one thing the mother does not have – a Y-chromosome. However, Professor R.J. Berry, of London University's Genetics Department, (a convinced Christian) states that an ovum in a woman with a particular type of chromosomal mutation develops without fertilization. The result would be a baby boy. Professor Berry does not claim that this had to be the way Mary conceived, or that, even if geneticists could never come up with a way of making parthenogenesis possible in humans, then his belief in the Virgin Birth would be shaken. 'The biological mechanisms for human parthenogenesis exist ... it would be improper in the light of our knowledge of genetics and embryology to say virgin births can never happen.'

3.4 A VARIETY OF VIEWS

Christians have held a variety of views about the true teaching of the Christian faith. Sadly, some of the differences between Christians have blown up into full scale bitterness and hatred. More light and less heat would be generated today if the circumstances and background of historical reforming movements were taken fully into account. For example, in Luther's day, the Roman Catholic Church was seen as corrupt and in need of reform. Initially, Luther never dreamed that he would split from it. Today, it sometimes appears that little has been learned from the sad divisions in the history of the Christian church. Richard Baxter's wise counsel needs to be heard again: 'In necessary things, unity; in doubtful things, liberty; in all things, charity.'

JEHOVAH'S WITNESSES

✠ DIFFERENCES
The seven Bible verses which explicitly state that Jesus is God and which are either ignored or misinterpreted by Jehovah's Witnesses are: John 1:1; John 1:18; John 20:28; 1 Timothy 3:16; Hebrews 1:8; 2 Peter 1:1 and 1 John 5:20.

✠ THE DAY THE CHURCH NEARLY BECAME JEHOVAH'S WITNESSES
At the Council of Nicea, Arius of Alexandria said that Jesus was *a* creation of the Father. His followers chanted, 'There was a time when the Son was not.'

The Christian church was saved from embracing Jehovah's Witnesses' beliefs when it affirmed that Jesus was 'from the substance of the Father, God from God, Light from Light, very God from very God, begotten not made, of the same substance as the Father...'

FIVE GLOBAL HERETICAL 'ISMS'

Theism is the belief in a personal God. In the Bible God is revealed as: Father (John 6:27); Son (Titus 2:13) and Holy Spirit (Acts 5:3,4).

✠ ATHEISM
The belief that there is no God. The Bible's estimate of atheists is summarized by the psalmist: 'The fool says in his heart, 'There is no God.'' Psalm 14:1

✠ POLYTHEISM
The belief in many gods.

✠ PANTHEISM
Pantheism teaches that all of nature is God.

✠ DEISM
Deism teaches that God created the universe and then abandoned it.

☩ FATALISM

Fatalism teaches that all events are pre-determined and cannot be altered by man. What will be will be.

VARIETY OF BELIEFS AMONG CHRISTIANS

Christians hold a wide range of beliefs about many important doctrinal topics.

☩ BAPTISM

Infant or adult? The big divide here is between those who believe in baptism of babies (infant baptism) and those who only

Make-do baptism at Glastonbury Festival, England, 1990.

allow the baptism of those teenagers and adults who have made a personal decision to trust Christ (believer's baptism). There are three views:

- **1. The sacramental view** Baptism is seen as a 'means of grace.' Augustine believed that baptism was essential to salvation. The baptized had their sins forgiven and were given Christ's new life. Lutherans thought that the preaching of God's word would bring alive the seed implanted at baptism.
- **2. The covenant view** Baptism is seen as a sign of a covenant relationship with God, just as circumcision was in the Old Testament. This view holds that baptism not only initiates the individual into the Christian church, but that it is also the sign and seal of God's grace of redemption.
- **3. The symbolic view** This view teaches that baptism is a confession, in public, of Christ as being one's personal Savior. It

sees baptism, usually by total immersion, as an appropriate symbol of God's work which has already united the believer to Jesus.

Karl Barth, the 20th-century Protestant Swiss theologian, attempted an ecumenical approach to baptism, in order to unite Christians. In this he said:

- Infant baptism: is out
- Adult baptism: is in
- Rebaptism: is out

Barth's approach did not gain wide support.

☩ SPEAKING IN TONGUES

The term 'speaking in tongues' has been used to describe two very different phenomena: glossolalia and xenoglossia.

SEVEN HISTORIC ECUMENICAL COUNCILS

Place	Date	Outcome
Nicea	325	Refuted Arianism, the belief that the Son of God is neither divine nor eternal. This breaks with the doctrine of the Trinity. Adopted Nicene Creed: Jesus is coeternal with the Father.
Constantinople	381	Condemned Apollinarian view that Jesus had no human will. Affirmed the deity of the Holy Spirit.
Ephesus	431	Condemned Pelagius' claim that man is not totally fallen; declared Nestorianism heretical (i.e. Jesus is two persons).
Chalcedon	451	Condemned Monophysite heresy that Jesus cannot have two natures in one person.
Constantinople	553	Condemned Theodore of Mopsuestia's writings as Nestorian.
Constantinople	680	Denied Monothelitism ('one will'). Believed that Christ had both divine and human wills.
Nicea	787	Legitimized veneration of icons.

Glossolalia This is the most common meaning of 'speaking in tongues.' This term is derived from two Greek words: *glōssai*, which means 'tongues' or 'languages,' and *lalein* which means 'to speak.'

It is practiced in some tribal religions and within some Christian denominations, notably charismatics, Mormons in past times, and Pentecostals.

What is glossolalia? Here is a selection of views:

- J. F. Jansen: 'A phenomenon of intense religious experience expressing itself in ecstatic speech.'
- J. G. Melton: 'To the outsider, hearing someone speaking in "tongues" is like hearing so much gibberish ... Glossolalia is the common prayer speech heard at Pentecostal churches.'
- The Interpreter's One-Volume Commentary on the Bible: 'The ecstatic utterance of emotionally agitated religious persons, consisting of a jumble of disjointed and largely unintelligible sounds. Those who speak in this way believe that they are moved directly by a divine spirit and their utterance is therefore quite spontaneous and unpremeditated.'
- The United Pentecostal Church International: 'One vital reason why God chose other tongues as the initial sign of receiving the Holy Ghost is that speaking in tongues is an immediate, external evidence. There are many other evidences of the operation of the Spirit of God in a person's life, but it is a matter of time before they are manifest ... Another reason why God chose other tongues as the initial sign of receiving the Spirit is that speaking in tongues is a uniform evidence. It applies to everyone, regardless of race, culture, or language.'

A person speaking in tongues is typically in a state of religious ecstasy and is often unable to understand the words that she/he is saying.

Many Christians who speak in tongues believe that they are speaking in an existing language. Some speculate that it is a heavenly tongue, that is, a language spoken by angels or by God. It was seen in the church at Corinth during the 1st century. It was experienced rarely during the history of Christianity until the 20th century when it has become more common.

Xenoglossia This is the ability to spontaneously speak a foreign language without first having learned or been exposed to it. This term is also derived from two Greek words: *xenos*, which means 'foreign' or 'foreigner', and *glōssai*, which means 'tongues' or 'languages.' Stories of xenoglossia are well known, particularly within the Pentecostal movement and from psychic research.

The viewpoint of Pentecostals and charismatics

A common belief among Pentecostals and charismatics is that the Holy Spirit, within the believer, uses glossolalia as a method of talking to God the Father in heaven. Some support this concept with the text of Romans 8:26 which says that the Holy Spirit makes intercessions for us with God with groans that words cannot express.

Baptism of the Holy Spirit

The United Pentecostal Church, and a few other Pentecostal denominations, believe that a person who sincerely repents of sin, and trusts in Jesus as Lord and Savior, is saved. At that time, or more likely at some later date, such a person will be 'baptized in the Holy Spirit,' and will receive from the Holy Spirit the gift of speaking 'in tongues.' This gift is considered proof of salvation.

- Tom Brown: 'The physical proof of the baptism in the Holy Spirit is the same evidence that the disciples had: speaking in tongues. You may have other evidences as well, but the one evidence you should have is speaking in tongues.'
- Assemblies of God, Statement of Fundamental Truths: 'The baptism of believers in the Holy Ghost is witnessed by the initial physical sign of speaking

ROMAN CATHOLICS

24 THINGS WHICH MAKE PROTESTANTS MAD!

1 Prayers for the dead. Started in the 4th century.
2 Veneration of angels and dead saints. Started AD 375.
3 The worship of Mary the mother of Jesus and the use of the term Mother of God, as applied to her. Originated in the Council of Ephesus in AD 431.
4 The doctrine of Purgatory. Formalized by Pope Gregory I in AD 593.
5 The Latin language as the language of prayer and worship in churches. Decreed by Pope Gregory I in AD 600.
6 Prayers directed to Mary or to dead saints. Started AD 600.
7 The title of pope, or universal bishop, which was first given to the bishop of Rome by Emperor Phocas in AD 610.
8 The kissing of the pope's feet, AD 709.
9 Worship of the cross, images and relics. Authorized in AD 788.
10 Canonization of dead saints. Started by Pope John XV in AD 995.
11 The Mass seen as a sacrifice. The idea was developed gradually; attendance made obligatory, 11th century.
12 The celibacy of the priesthood. This was decreed in 1079.
13 The rosary. This was introduced by Peter the Hermit in 1090.
14 The inquisition of heretics. This was instituted by the Council of Verona in 1184.
15 The sale of indulgences, commonly regarded as a purchase of forgiveness and a permit to indulge in sin, began in 1190.
16 The dogma of transubstantiation. Decreed by Pope Innocent III in 1215.
17 Confession of sins to the priest at least once a year. This was instituted by Pope Innocent III in the Lateran Council, 1215.
18 The adoration of the host (consecrated wafer). Formulated by Pope Honorius in 1220.
19 The Bible was forbidden to be read by laymen and placed in the Index of Forbidden Books by the Council of Toledo in 1229.
20 At the Lord's Supper, the cup of wine was forbidden to be given to the laity in the Council of Constance in 1414.
21 The doctrine of Seven Sacraments. Affirmed in 1439.
22 Six apocryphal books were added to the Bible by the Council of Trent in 1546.
23 The immaculate conception of the Virgin Mary. Proclaimed by Pope Pius IX in 1854.
24 The dogma of papal infallibility. Decreed by Pope Pius IX in 1870.

with other tongues as the Spirit of God gives them utterance ...'
- **Rev William Branham**: 'God wants to call us together in a unity of power to bring back the fullness of the Holy Ghost into the church again, with all the spiritual gifts in operation in every local body. They should be in full operation in every body, every church.'

Summary of different views

Pentecostals and charismatics generally believe that speaking in tongues today is as much a gift of the Holy Spirit as it was during the time of the apostles and is a necessary sign of the presence of the Spirit in a person's life.

Some non-Pentecostals believe that the various gifts of the Spirit, including the gift of tongues, ended with the death of the apostles.

Other non-Pentecostals believe that speaking in tongues is a gift of the Spirit, given to some Christians, but is not an essential, or even important, indication of salvation.

MARTIN LUTHER

✛ MOST EFFICACIOUS RELICS

The relics inside Castle Church, where Luther posted his 95 *Theses*, were reckoned to earn a pilgrim remission of 1,902,202 years and 270 days.

✛ THE MOST REFORMING SET OF THESES

One of the pivotal points of the Reformation was the day that Martin Luther nailed his 95 *Theses* to the church door in Wittenberg. In them Luther maintained that the Bible alone, not Popes and councils, was true and reliable.

Part 4

CHRISTIAN EXPERIENCE

4.1
CONVERSIONS

4.2
PROPHECIES

4.3
VISIONS

4.1 CONVERSIONS

Many people who have not been brought up in evangelical circles are somewhat suspicious of, if not outright implacably opposed to, all talk of 'born again' Christians, or, 'the second birth', or, 'being born again.' They associate such language with mass evangelism where they fear that gullible crowds are swamped in a tide of emotionalism generated by a charismatic, fast-talking evangelist.

But the phrase 'born again' is first used in the Bible in a totally different context. Jesus told one of Israel's top religious leaders, in a private, nocturnal conversation, that he needed to be born again. 'I tell you the truth, no one can see the kingdom of God unless he is born again' (John 3:3).

William Carey.

✥ AUGUSTINE

'Then I ran back to where Alypius was sitting; for, when I left him, I had left the apostle's book lying there. I picked it up, opened it, and silently read the passage [Romans 13:13-14] I first set eyes on: "Let us behave decently, as in the daytime, not in orgies and drunkenness, nor in sexual immorality and debauchery, not in dissension and jealousy. Rather clothe yourselves with the Lord Jesus Christ, and do not think about how to gratify the desires of the sinful nature." I didn't want to read any further, and it wasn't necessary. As I reached the end of the sentence, the light of peace seemed to shine on my heart, and every shadow of doubt disappeared.'
CONFESSIONS, AUGUSTINE, BOOK 8, SECTION 12

✥ WILLIAM BOOTH

William Booth's name became synonymous with some of the most amazing conversion stories in the annals of Christianity. However, Booth's own conversion was straightforward and unemotional. He was wandering home at about 11:00pm one night in 1844, when quite suddenly his soul was filled with God's Spirit. It was like Saul's Damascus Road experience. He experienced the light of God's forgiveness in his heart as he confessed his sins and knew that he was now a follower of the Lord Jesus Christ.

✥ WILLIAM CAREY

In 1779 a National Day of Prayer was called, as England was at war with Spain and France. William Carey went to a prayer meeting in the small meeting-room of the local Dissenting congregation. One of the members read Hebrews 13:13: 'Let us go forth therefore unto him without the camp, bearing his reproach.' The words were familiar to William, but now they found a deep resonance in his heart. The world was still rejecting Christ, but William knew that he had to commit himself, not intellectually but with his heart. It came as the climax of several weeks of searching, at last he realized that Christ had found him and given him peace.

✤ AMY CARMICHAEL

Amy Carmichael, the Irish missionary to India, was converted after hearing Anna Bartlett Warner's hymn *Jesus Loves Me* at a children's mission in Yorkshire, England.

✤ CHARLES 'CHUCK' COLSON

After Charles Colson had served a prison sentence for his part in the Watergate break-in and cover up, he was racked with doubts about Christianity. However, he could not get the phrase 'Jesus Christ is God' out of his head. In the best way he knew he surrendered to God and asked him to take over his life. But he had no certainty about his faith and spent the next week studying the Bible. During this time he felt as if he made massive spiritual progress in his understanding of Christianity. Then he was able to articulate a prayer which he thought would never pass his lips: he told Jesus that he believed in him, and accepted him. Asking Jesus to come into his life, he committed his life to his Lord.

Colson immediately had a sense of God's comfort and the knowledge that he could now face life with Christ in a totally new and reformed way. Colson now knew what it was to be born again in Christ.

✤ ELIZABETH FRY

'I think my feelings that night ... were the most exalted I remember ... suddenly my mind felt clothed with light, as with a garment and I felt silenced before God; I cried with the heavenly feeling of humility and repentance.'
MEMOIR OF ELIZABETH FRY

✤ C. S. LEWIS

C. S. Lewis was alone in his room at Magdalen College, Oxford, when he found that his thoughts kept returning to the subject of God, whom, he says, he did not want to meet. In 1929 he knelt down and

acknowledged that God was indeed God. He felt as if he was the most 'dejected and reluctant convert in all England.'

At this stage Lewis thought of God as being other than human, and he did not think about Jesus Christ being God incarnate.

As he saw the truth of Jesus being man and God, he again put up resistance, just as before, until he was at last prepared to admit that Jesus was God.

This final step in Lewis' Christian conversion took place while he traveled on a bus to visit Whipsnade Zoo. It was a lovely sunny morning. When he left Oxford he did not

Charles 'Chuck' Colson.

believe that Jesus Christ was the Son of God. By the time that he arrived at Whipsnade he did believe that Jesus Christ was the Son of God. Yet Lewis recalls that he had not spent the journey deep in thought, nor were any great emotional feelings linked to this change of heart. Lewis felt that some people are very unemotional about some of the most important events in their lives. He likened his conversion experience to being like a man who, after a long sleep, still lies motionless.

✚ MARTIN LUTHER

'Night and day I pondered until I saw the connection between the justice of God and the statement that "the just shall live by his faith" (Romans 1:17). Then I grasped that the justice of God is that righteousness by which, through grace and sheer mercy, God justifies us through faith. Thereupon I felt myself to be reborn and to have gone through open doors into paradise. The whole of Scripture took on a new meaning, and whereas before the "justice of God" had filled me with hate, now it became to me inexpressibly sweet in greater love. This passage of Paul became to me a gate to heaven.'

MARTIN LUTHER

✚ JUSTIN MARTYR

After meeting an old man by the sea who explained the weakness of Plato's philosophy and spoke about prophets more ancient than Greek philosophers who spoke about the truth about God and prophesied about Christ's coming, Justin Martyr wrote: 'Straightway a flame was kindled in my soul; and a love of the prophets, and of those men who are friends of Christ, possessed me; and whilst revolving his words in my mind, I found this philosophy alone to be safe and profitable.'

✚ ST PATRICK

'I was 16 years old and knew not the true God and was carried away captive; but in that strange land [Ireland] the Lord opened my unbelieving eyes, and although late I called my sins to mind, and was converted with my whole heart to the Lord my God, who regarded my low estate, had pity on my youth and ignorance, and consoled me as a father consoles his children ... Well every day I used to look after sheep and I used to pray often during the day, the love of God and fear of him increased more and more in me and my faith began to grow and my spirit stirred up, so that in one day I would pray as many as a hundred times and nearly as many at night. Even when I was staying out in the woods or on the mountain, I used to rise before dawn for prayer, in snow and frost and rain, and I felt no ill effect and there was no slackness in me. As I now realize, it was because the Spirit was glowing in me.'

PATRICK'S CONFESSION

✚ C. H. SPURGEON

'I sometimes think I might have been in darkness and despair until now had it not been for the goodness of God in sending a snowstorm, one Sunday morning, while I was going to a certain place to worship. When I could go no further, I turned down a side street, and came to a little Primitive Methodist Chapel. In that chapel there may have been a dozen or 15 people. I had heard of the Primitive Methodists, how they sang so loudly that they made people's heads ache; but that did not matter to me. I wanted to know how I might be saved, and if they could tell me that, I did not care how much they made my head ache. The minister did not come that morning; he was snowed up, I suppose. At last, a very thin-looking man, a shoemaker, or tailor, or something of that sort, went up into the pulpit to preach. Now, it is well that preachers should be instructed, but this

Metropolitan Tabernacle, South London, where Charles Spurgeon preached.

'I saw at once the way of salvation. I knew not what else he said – I did not take much notice of it – I was so possessed with that one thought. There and then the cloud was gone, the darkness had rolled away, and that moment I saw the sun. Oh, that somebody had told me this before, "Trust Christ, and you shall be saved."'

C. H. Spurgeon's Autobiography

✠ JOHN WESLEY

'Bristol, 1788: About the middle of the discourse, when there was on every side attention still as night, a vehement noise arose, none could tell whence, and shot like lightning through the whole congregation. The terror and confusion was inexpressible. You might have imagined it was a city taken by storm. The people rushed upon each other with the utmost violence, the benches were broken in pieces, and nine tenths of the congregation appeared to be struck with the same panic. In about six minutes the storm ceases.

'It is the strangest incident of the kind I ever remember, and I believe none can account for it without supposing some

man was really stupid. He was obliged to stick to his text, for the simple reason that he had little else to say. The text was, "Look unto me, and be ye saved, all the ends of the earth."

'Then the good man followed up his text in this way: "Look unto Me; I am sweatin' great drops of blood. Look unto Me; I am hangin' on the cross. Look unto Me, I am dead and buried. Look unto Me, I am sitting at the Father's right hand. O poor sinner, look unto Me! Look unto Me!"

'Then he looked at me under the gallery, and I dare-say, with so few present, he knew me to be a stranger. Just fixing his eyes on me, as if he knew all my heart, he said, "Young man, you look very miserable." Well, I did, but I had not been accustomed to have remarks made from the pulpit on my personal appearance before. However, it was a good blow, and it struck right home. He continued, "and you always will be miserable – miserable in life and miserable in death – if you don't obey my text; but if you obey now, this moment you will be saved." Then lifting up his hands, he shouted, as only a Primitive Methodist could do, "Young man, look to Jesus Christ. Look! Look! Look! You have nothing to do but to look and live."

John Wesley, founder of Methodism.

supernatural influence. Satan fought, lest his kingdom should be delivered up.'
THE JOURNAL OF JOHN WESLEY, 3RD MARCH 1788

REVIVALS

✠ FIRST USED
The word 'revival' was first used with specifically Christian connotations in 1702.

✠ MOST LONG-LASTING
The revivals in 18th-century England led by John and Charles Wesley and George Whitefield, and those in America strongly supported by George Whitefield and led by Jonathan Edwards probably had the greatest long-term effect.

✠ FREQUENCY OF REVIVALS
There has been a major revival somewhere in the world every 50 years since the 18th century.

✠ PENTECOSTAL CHURCHES
The 20th-century Pentecostal Churches trace their origin to the Azusa Street Revival of Los Angeles in 1906.

✠ EMPHASIS ON CHARISMATIC GIFTS
The Toronto Blessing
In January 1994, a little church on the end of a runway at Pearson International Airport in Toronto came to the world's attention as a place where God chose to meet with his people. As a result of this divine visitation, the members of what was at that time the Toronto Airport Vineyard were thrust into ministry to thousands of people worldwide.

The Toronto Blessing is a transferable anointing. In its most visible form it overcomes worshipers with outbreaks of laughter, weeping, groaning, shaking, falling, 'drunkenness,' and even behaviors that have been described as a 'cross between a jungle and a farmyard.' Of greater significance, however, are the changed lives.

The 'renewal' came to what was then the Toronto Airport Vineyard through visiting pastor Randy Clark of St Louis, Missouri.

In early September of 1995, cumulative attendance at what was later to become known as the Toronto Airport Christian Fellowship was about 600,000, including approximately 20,000 Christian leaders and 200,000 first-time visitors.

The effects of the Toronto Blessing quickly became international in scope. In the United Kingdom, the renewal broke out in May of 1994 at an Anglican Church, Holy Trinity, Brompton, and within a year of the outpouring, an estimated four thousand churches representing the main denominations in the United Kingdom had been touched.

The Toronto Blessing has not only spread to England, but to Africa, Australia, Cambodia, China, Czechoslavakia, Denmark, Finland, Germany, Guinea, Guyana, Holland, Hungary, Iceland, India, Indonesia, Israel, Japan, Kenya, Korea, mainland Malaysia, Norway, Romania, Russia, Singapore, South Sweden, Switzerland, Taiwan, Thailand, New Zealand, Zimbabwe and many other places.

The Toronto Airport Christian Fellowship (TACF) includes in its statement of faith: 'We believe the Holy Spirit lives in us as believers and brings love, joy, peace, patience, kindness, goodness, faithfulness, humility and self-control into our lives. He works in and through us with His charismatic gifts.'

.2 PROPHECIES

In the Bible 'prophecy' covers a wide spectrum of topics, from preaching to foretelling a specific event. When the great Old Testament prophets such as Isaiah and Jeremiah called out, 'Thus says the Lord ...' they delivered topical 'sermons' which they had been inspired by God to deliver. Joel's famous prophecy was dramatically fulfilled on the Day of Pentecost: 'And afterwards I will pour out my Spirit on all people. Your sons and daughters will prophesy, your old men will dream dreams ...' (Joel 2:28).

The Bible gives many specific prophecies about the end of the world, and Jesus says: 'No one knows about that day or hour, not even the angels in heaven, nor the Son, but only the Father. Be on guard! Be alert! You do not know when that time will come' (Mark 13:32-33).

ABOUT THE END OF THE WORLD

1532
'There are rumors that the world will end in 1532. I hope it won't be long ... the world cannot last much longer.'
MARTIN LUTHER

1830: THE START OF THE FINAL OUTPOURING OF THE HOLY SPIRIT
Edward Irving, one of the forerunners of the modern Pentecostal movement, allowed speaking in tongues in his meetings. He believed that all Christians should be baptized in the Holy Spirit and as evidence they would speak in tongues. He also expected that there would be prophecies and healings. In 1830 there were claims that people in the west of Scotland showed such signs. Irving thought that this marked the start of the final outpouring of the Holy Spirit before the return of Jesus.

1866
Jonathan Edwards along with other Protestant thinkers expected that the 'papal beast' would be destroyed in 1866.

1867
Edward Irving predicted that the Millennium (thousand year reign) would commence in 1867.

1992
Edgar C. Whisenaut, retired NASA engineer, predicted the end would come in May of 1992.

PROPHETS AMONG THE REFORMERS

LUTHER AND PROPHECY
'One may prophesy new things but not things that go beyond the bounds of faith.'
MARTIN LUTHER

'If you wish to prophesy, do it in such a way that it does not go beyond faith so that your prophesying can be in harmony with the peculiar quality of faith.'
MARTIN LUTHER

'My dear brethren, do your best to become prophets, men of the Spirit; otherwise, your theology will not avail you one groat. Contemplate your God from close to, not from a distance.'
PHILIP MELANCHTHON (1497-1560), GERMAN THEOLOGIAN, GREEK EXPERT, AND FRIEND OF MARTIN LUTHER

PROPHECY AND GLOBAL TRENDS

Robert I. Holmes, contributing editor of *Storm-Harvest Ministries*, made the following prophecies in 1998: 'Great tribulation is coming upon the earth and many parts of the world will be thrown into turmoil. Japan will buckle further, China will begin to flex her well-toned muscles. Russia will continue to escape her debt, and throw money at things she should not. This will be at the expense of millions of common citizens. There are about to be released, plagues on the earth – mutations of existing and prevalent viruses, revival of those defeated and new strains. Watch for a fourth generation of AIDS/HIV and for communicable cancer. The only place of healing will be found in the church.'

PROPHECIES FROM CATHOLIC SAINTS AND MYSTICS

✠ BROTHER JOHN OF THE CLEFT ROCK

(*14th century*)
'Towards the end of the world, tyrants and hostile mobs will rob the Church and the clergy of all their possessions and will afflict and martyr them. Those who heap the most abuse upon them will be held in high esteem.

'At that time, the Pope with his cardinals will have to flee Rome in tragic circumstances to a place where they will be unknown. The Pope will die a cruel death in his exile. The sufferings of the Church will be much greater than at any previous time in her history.'

✠ VENERABLE BARTHOLOMEW HOLZHAUSER

(*17th century, Germany*)
'These are evil times, a century full of dangers and calamities. Heresy is everywhere, and the followers of heresy are in power almost everywhere. Bishops, prelates, and priests say that they are doing their duty, that they are vigilant, and that they live as befits their state in life. In like manner, therefore, they all seek excuses. But God will permit a great evil against His Church: heretics and tyrants will come suddenly and unexpectedly; they will break into the Church while bishops, prelates, and priests are asleep. They will enter Italy and lay Rome waste; they will burn down the churches and destroy everything.'

✠ SISTER ELENA AIELLO

(*20th century, Italy*)
'An unforeseen fire will descend over the whole earth, and a great part of humanity will be destroyed. This will be a time of despair for the impious: with shouts and satanic blasphemy, they will beg to be covered by the mountains, and they will try to seek refuge in caverns, but to no avail. Those who remain will find God's mercy, power, and protection, while all who refuse to repent of their sins will perish in a sea of fire!'

.3 VISIONS

In classic Christian thought the greatest vision anyone can have is the vision of God, also called the beatific vision. The concept that the ultimate destiny of the righteous is that they should see God can be traced back to the Bible: see Psalm 17:15; Revelation 22:3-4. The idea of the beatific vision was ignored by the Reformers, as they considered it to be the preserve of the monasteries. In doing this they neglected an important part of the Bible's teaching on hope and the second coming of Christ.

In the Middle Ages the Christians in the West defined the beatific vision as the direct, intuitive vision of the essence of God. This doctrine underlined the truth that God himself is the ultimate goal of human life and that in heaven the redeemed will have an immediate relationship with God. Julian of Norwich's account of her visions, in the first book to be written in English by a woman, struggles to depict this unimaginable hope.

✠ PETER'S VISION

Outside Rome, on the Appian Way stands a little chapel known as *Domine, quo vadis?* – 'Lord, whither goest thou?' Bishop Lightfoot, among others, is inclined to believe the story that the Christians at Rome came to Peter at the start of the persecution and begged him to flee from the city.

'Peter gave in to their pleas. When Peter reached the place where the chapel stands, Jesus Christ met him in the middle of a dark night. The apostle asked his Lord, as he had done before, "What do you want me to do?" The Lord answered him, "I go to Rome, to be crucified again." Peter was quick to understand the meaning behind this rebuke. He returned to Rome and told the Christian brethren what he had seen, and then glorified God by his death, as the Lord had foretold that he would, when he said, "Another shall gird thee and carry thee wither thou wouldest not."'

AMBROSE, *EPISTLE* 21

✠ CONSTANTINE'S VISION

In 312, before engaging Maxentius in battle, the Roman emperor Constantine prayed to the 'Supreme God' for help. Then he was given a sign, a cross in the noonday sky 'above the sun' with the words, 'Conquer by this.' That night, Constantine had a dream in which Christ told him to use the 'Chi-Rho' sign, the first two letters of Christ's name in Greek, 'as a safeguard in all engagements with his enemies.' The historian Lactantius records that Constantine ordered that this 'Chi-Rho' sign be written on the shields of all his soldiers. Constantine then defeated Maxentius as he marched on Rome. At the traditional place of this encounter an inscription reads: 'In this sign you will conquer. Good Christian, do not pass the spot without recognizing Jesus Christ our Redeemer. Praise be to Jesus Christ forever and ever. Amen.'

✠ JEROME'S DREAM

In Antioch Jerome had a most disturbing dream in AD 374. In it Christ was scourging him and accusing him, 'You are a Ciceronian, and not a Christian.' Jerome was convicted that he had devoted too much time to studying the pagan classics and had ignored the Christian writings. As a consequence of this dream Jerome became a hermit, learned Hebrew, and went on to write the *Vulgate* translation of the Bible.

It was in AD 382 that Pope Damascus I commissioned Jerome to produce an authoritative translation of the Bible. At the time the custom was to translate from the Greek Old Testament and the Latin translations of the New Testament. Jerome, however, translated directly from the Hebrew Old Testament and the Greek New Testament texts.

✠ DROPS OF GENTLE RAIN

Hildegard of Bingen had a beyond consciousness experience (known as *excessus mentis* or, *exstasis*) in which she states, 'I saw a wonderfully mystical vision which made my whole womb convulse and cut dead all my other physical powers of sense. I received knowledge in some other way, as if I no longer knew myself. Like drops of gentle rain God's inspiration filled my mind, just as the Holy Spirit came into John the Evangelist when he suckled deep revelations from the breast of Jesus.'

HILDEGARD OF BINGEN (1098-1179), GERMAN ABBESS, KNOWN AS 'SIBYL OF THE RHINE'

✠ A WAKING DREAM

'There are some natures to whom the great spiritual world of the unseen is always present as the background of life. It was so with Shakespeare. It was so also with Bunyan, though in a different way.

'Then blossomed into shape his wonderful power of dreaming waking dreams. One day as he was passing into the field, still with some fears in his heart, suddenly this sentence fell into his soul, "'Thy righteousness is in heaven': and methought withal I

Jerome.

saw with the eye of my soul, Jesus Christ at God's right hand. I saw, moreover, that it was not my good frame of heart that made my righteousness better, nor yet my bad frame that made my righteousness worse; for my righteousness was Jesus Christ Himself, the same yesterday, today, and for ever. Now did my chains fall from my legs indeed; I was loosed from my afflictions and irons. Oh, methought, Christ! Christ! there was nothing but Christ that was before my eyes! Now Christ was all; all my wisdom, all my righteousness, all my sanctification, and all my redemption!"'

JOHN BROWN, *JOHN BUNYAN*

✠ DRAWN SWORD VISION

'As I was walking in my chambers, [in 1664] with my eye to the Lord, "I saw the angel of the Lord with a glittering drawn sword stretched southward, as though the court had been all on fire." Not long afterwards the wars broke out with Holland, the sickness broke forth, and later the fire of London; so the Lord's sword was drawn indeed.'

THE JOURNAL OF GEORGE FOX (LONDON, 1852), VOL. II

✠ 'I DID SEE THE GREAT GOD HIMSELF'

George Frideric Handel (1685-1759), wrote his oratorio, *The Messiah* 'in just 24 days. He worked on his masterpiece night and day and hardly slept or ate. One day his servant opened the door to find Handel at

Handel as a child.

his work, with tears streaming down his face. Handel looked up and cried out, "I did think I did see all Heaven before me, and the great God Himself."'

✤ THE HAZELNUT VISION

'God showed me in a vision a little thing, the quantity of a hazelnut, lying in the palm of my hand; and, to my under-standing, it was round as any ball. In this little thing, I saw three parts: the first is that God made it. The second is that he loves it. The third is that God keeps it.

'I saw all-thing God had made. It is great and fair and large and good. But the cause why it showed so little to my sight was because I saw it in the presence of him that is its Maker. For to a soul that sees the Maker of all-thing, all that is made seems full little. God made all-thing that is made for love, and through the same love it is kept and ever shall be without end. For God is all-thing that is good, and the goodness that all-thing has is he. Therefore he is in all-thing. God doth all-thing, be it never so little. And nothing is done by hap nor by chance, but by the endless foresight of the wisdom of God.'

LADY JULIAN, RECLUSE AT NORWICH, 1373,
REVELATIONS OF DIVINE LOVE

✤ A VISIONARY'S EXPERIENCE DESCRIBED

'She was swept away into an indescribable light, and in this divine light she saw the elements and the creatures and the things which are made from them, both small and great, stand out in such brilliance, that each of them, however small, appeared a hundred times more brilliant than the sun – even the smallest grain of corn or pebble. And the light of the present world compared with this brilliance would have seemed dark like the moon when she is covered by a dark cloud. And created things appeared so clearly in this radiance that each could be distinguished by its quality; a green grain, a red rose, etc. But among all the elements and created things the earth was the most splendid. And this because God took his body from the earth; and because during the Lord's Passion the earth was drenched with the blood of the Savior. All this was in the Man – Christ.

AGNES BLANNBEKIN OF VIENNA,
A 14TH-CENTURY GERMAN VISIONARY

Part 5

CHRISTIAN GROUPS

5.1
TRADITIONAL
GROUPS

5.2
MODERN
GROUPS

5.3
MISSION GROUPS

5.4
RELIEF
ORGANIZATIONS

5.5
SERVICE
GROUPS

5.1 TRADITIONAL GROUPS

About 33% of the world's population regard themselves as Christian. This percentage has been stable for decades. However, if present trends continue, the second most popular religion, Islam, will become the dominant religion of the world during the 21st century.

Most Americans have some kind of affiliation with one of the traditional Christian denominations. In the US about nine out of ten people are happy to be known as Christians. This proportion has been dropping very slowly in recent years, mainly due to the sudden increase in non-theists, such as agnostics, atheists, and humanists. Other factors are the proliferation of new groups like the New Age movement.

MULTIPLICITY OF DENOMINATIONS

Christianity in North America is a severely divided faith consisting of over 1,200 formal Christian organizations.

✣ THE CHRISTIAN FAMILY TREE
The main families and communities within Christianity, particularly those in the Middle East, Europe, and North America may be categorized into various 'families' or traditions. The following descriptions are compiled from material which the denominations themselves use to explain their history and teaching.

THE ORTHODOX FAMILY

Orthodox Christians are organically the same congregation (or *ecclesia*) as that born at the outpouring of the Holy Spirit in Jerusalem at Pentecost. They are a direct continuation from the apostles by the laying on of hands from each generation of priests to the next.

The Orthodox Christian has been baptized in the name of the Holy Trinity and follows the ideals and beliefs of both the Scriptures and sacred tradition. He believes in a living and loving God, whose grace protects and guides him in the path of redemption. He believes that God has revealed himself in the Bible through the prophets and especially in the person of Jesus Christ, His only-begotten Son who is man's Savior. He especially believes in the incarnation of Christ as God-Man, in his crucifixion and resurrection, in his gospel and commandments, and in the world to come.

The Eastern Orthodox family, its authority centered in the cities of Antioch, Alexandria and Constantinople, split from

the Western Catholic tradition in AD 1054. They reject the authority of the pope and are governed by patriarchs who have equal authority and are in communion with each other. The Eastern Orthodox family does not demand celibacy of its priests (as long as they are married before their ordination). Monks who are celibate are the only members who attain the office of bishop. This family does not recognize the part of the Chalcedonian Creed that states that the Holy Spirit proceeds from the Son and the Father.

Rouen Cathedral, France.

THE (ROMAN) CATHOLIC FAMILY

The Catholic Church is the world's largest, and Christianity's oldest, religious body. Her 900 million members inhabit the width and breadth of the earth, comprising almost one-fifth of the total human population.

DISTINCTIVE BELIEFS OF ROMAN CATHOLICS

The Church

Catholics believe that their Church is the one true Church of Jesus Christ. They, for many reasons, believe it is the only Christian Church that goes back in history to the time of Christ. They also believe it is the only Christian Church which possesses the invincible unity, the intrinsic holiness, the continual universality and the indisputable apostolicity which Christ said would distinguish his true Church: the apostles and early Church Fathers all professed membership in this same Catholic Church. So Ignatius of Antioch could write, 'Where the Bishop is, there let the multitude of believers be; even as where Jesus is, there is the Catholic Church.'

The Pope

Catholics believe that Peter the apostle was the first pope and that under certain circumstances the pope is infallible in his teachings.

FOUR CONDITIONS

In order for the pope to be infallible on a particular statement, four conditions must apply:

1. He must be speaking *ex cathedra* ... that is, 'from the Chair' of Peter, or in other words, officially, as head of the entire Church;
2. the decision must be for the whole Church;
3. it must be on a matter of faith or morals;
4. the pope must have the intention of making a final decision on a teaching of faith or morals, so that it is to be held by all the faithful. It must be interpretive, not originative; the pope has no authority to originate new doctrine.

Sacraments

Catholics believe in seven sacraments, while Protestants accept only two.

Catholics believe Christ instituted seven; because the apostles and Church Fathers believed in seven; the second Ecumenical Council of Lyons (1274)

ANGLICAN FAMILY

The English church broke with Rome in the 16th century and became the Anglican tradition when Henry VIII saw the opportunity for an independent church that would give him his desired divorce and financial freedom for battle. *The Thirty-nine Articles of Religion* and *The Book of Common Prayer* established a separate liturgical tradition.

After Henry VIII initiated a church independent of Rome the Church of England spread throughout the British Empire where sister churches sprang up. These churches, while autonomous in their government, are bound together by tradition, Scripture, and the inheritance they have received from the Church of England. They together make up the Anglican Communion, a body headed spiritually by the Archbishop of Canterbury and having some 80 million members, making it the second largest Christian body in the world.

High Beach Church, rural England.

defined seven; and because the Ecumenical Council of Trent (1545-1563) confirmed seven.

The traditional Christian definition of a sacrament is 'an outward sign instituted by Christ to give grace' to the soul. When this special grace – distinct from ordinary, inspirational grace – is imparted to the soul, the Holy Spirit of God is imparted to the soul, imbuing it with divine life, and uniting it to Christ.

THE SEVEN SACRAMENTS

1. BAPTISM: the sacrament of spiritual rebirth through which people are made children of God and heirs of heaven.
2. CONFIRMATION: the sacrament which confers the Holy Spirit to make us strong and perfect Christians and soldiers of Jesus Christ.
3. The EUCHARIST: the sacrament, also known as Holy Communion, which nourishes the soul with the true flesh and blood, soul and divinity of Jesus, under the appearance, or sacramental veil, of bread and wine.

4. PENANCE: the sacrament, also known as confession, through which Christ forgives sin and restores the soul to grace.
5. EXTREME UNCTION: the sacrament, sometimes called the Last Anointing, which strengthens the sick and sanctifies the dying.
6. HOLY ORDERS: the sacrament of ordination which empowers priests to offer the Holy Sacrifice of the Mass, administer the sacraments, and officiate over all the other proper affairs of the Church.
7. MATRIMONY: the sacrament which unites a man and woman in a holy and indissoluble bond.

'The Word of Christ and the example of the Apostles attest both to the validity and the efficacy of the seven Sacraments of the Catholic Church. In truth, every one of them is an integral part of Christ's plan for man's eternal salvation.'
PAUL WHITCOMB

✠ THE EPISCOPAL CHURCH

After the immigration to North America and the American Revolutionary War, the Anglican Church in North America became known, in 1787, as the Protestant Episcopal Church in the US.

Today the Episcopal Church is the American branch of the Anglican Communion, which is an inheritor of 2,000 years of catholic and apostolic tradition dating from Christ himself, rooted in the Church of England.

Today the Episcopal Church has between two and three million members in the United States, Mexico, and Central America, all of which are under the jurisdiction of the Presiding Bishop of the Episcopal Church.

For more than two decades the American Episcopal Church has ordained women to the priesthood. In 1988 the Diocese of Massachusetts elected the first Anglican woman bishop, Barbara Harris.

LUTHERAN FAMILY

Martin Luther, with the active support of the German princes, split away from the Roman Catholic Church and formed the Lutheran Church. In 1530, the Augsburg Confession was published and became the standard that congregations used to justify their independent existence. They were then known as 'confessing churches.' Luther and the Augsburg Confession taught that salvation is by grace through faith, rather than works and faith, and that the Bible is the rule of faith and sole authority for doctrine. Luther, unlike many other reformers, placed great emphasis on the sacramental liturgy and understood the Lord's Supper as consubstantiation (Christ present but the bread and wine not changed). This contrasted with the Roman Catholic tradition of transubstantiation (the elements changed into Christ's essence). Luther's translation of the Bible into the German vernacular (1532-34) became the standard for the German language and sparked the use of the vernacular in the Lutheran liturgy. Through Luther, many new hymns came into use and changed the complexion of the liturgy.

REFORMED-PRESBYTERIAN FAMILY

The force behind this family is the Frenchman, John Calvin, who established the Reformed Church in Geneva, Switzerland, in the 1540s. The Reformed Churches distinguish themselves from the other Christian families by their theology (Reformed) and the church government (Presbyterian). Calvin derived his Reformed theology from the major premise of God's sovereignty in creation and salvation. He taught that God predestined some to salvation and that atonement is limited to those whom God has elected. In the Lord's Supper, God, who is present, can be apprehended by faith, but not through the bread and the wine.

METHODIST FAMILY

Included in this family are the Moravian Church, the Swedish Evangelical Churches and the Methodist (Wesleyan) Churches. As a movement of pietism, these Churches reacted against what they perceived as the rigidity of the systematic doctrine of some Lutheran and Calvinist theologians. They came to be characterized by their emphasis on the individual spiritual experience of Christians, giving expression to their faith in hymns, testimony and evangelical zeal. Through the early work of Philip Jacob Spener and August Herrman Francke, their work rejuvenated the Moravian Church in 1727, influenced John Wesley and helped establish the Swedish Evangelical Church. In their work they were open to traditional practices and beliefs and sought life within the forms of the traditional Churches. Methodists do not go along with Calvinist teachings on predestination and irresistible grace.

Free-Church congregation, England,

In 1784 the Methodists in America formed the Methodist Episcopal Church.

✠ UNITED METHODIST CHURCH

In 1729 in England, a small group of Oxford University students were ridiculed as 'Bible Bigots,' the 'Holy Club' and 'Methodists' because they spent so much time in methodical prayer and Bible reading. Led by John and Charles Wesley, the students held their ground against jeering students and went out to preach and pray with those considered to be the dregs of English society. John Wesley never wanted to split from the Anglican Church, even after he had been barred from preaching in Anglican churches. But after he became 'an apostle to the [British] nation,' following his own conversion, he had to care for the numerous new Christians. The Methodist organization came into being to meet this need.

The United Methodist Church is the result of the 1939 merger of three Methodist bodies (Methodist Episcopal, Methodist Episcopal South and Methodist Protestant churches), and a 1968 union of the Evangelical United Brethren and the Methodist churches.

FREE-CHURCH FAMILY

Some Reformers of the 16th century, unlike Luther and Calvin who taught a close relationship with the state, advocated a complete break with the state Church. Many of their other teachings were similar to the doctrine of the Reformation, but the way they organized the government of their churches was very different.

The Mennonites, the Amish, the Brethren, the Quakers and the Free Church of Brethren make up this family of Free-Church Christians. Because many of them cut off completely from the government of their country they suffered severe persecution. This resulted in many fleeing from Europe to North America where they established congregations.

Many members of these groups, particularly Quakers and Mennonites, are pacifists; at the same time, they are highly active in their work to prevent war and in their relief efforts worldwide.

✠ THE MENNONITE CHURCH

The Mennonite Church is a Christian denomination of more than 1,100 congregations in North America who follow the teachings of Jesus and are committed to God's way of peace. Like Lutherans, who were named after Martin Luther, Mennonites were nicknamed after an early Dutch leader, Menno Simons.

This movement began in the 16th century within the Protestant Reformation in Europe. A small group of earnest young believers held that the reformers Martin Luther and Ulrich Zwingli had not gone far enough. Conrad Grebel led this group in an attempt to recover New Testament Christianity as they baptized one another and verbalized their faith in Jesus Christ at Zurich, Switzerland, in January 1525.

Fired by their new faith, the believers began to evangelize and the movement rapidly spread to South Germany and the Netherlands. The official Churches immediately opposed the movement and scoffed at Mennonites as 'Anabaptizers,' which literally means re-baptizers. Despite their

…urch
…ngregation,
…hina.

strong appeal to Scripture in support of their position the state would not tolerate the Mennonites because in essence they defied the government-run church. In a short time, many were martyred. Over the next two generations thousands more died gruesome deaths at the hands of their persecutors.

Today, nearly half of the Mennonite family is to be found in Africa, Asia, and Latin America, which is also where the Church is experiencing the most rapid growth. The Mennonite Church exists in 61 countries around the world and has more than one million members.

BAPTIST FAMILY

American Baptists trace their roots back to the continental Free-Church family, and especially to British Puritanism. Most Baptist groups place more emphasis on the Scriptures than on any particular historic Christian creed. They insist on baptism by immersion which must be administered only to believing and confessing adults. They are certain that salvation is a gift of God's grace, and that people must exercise their free will to receive it.

There are more Baptists in America than anywhere else in the world. On average there are 210 members for each Baptist church.

INDEPENDENT FUNDAMENTALIST FAMILY

Following the lead of Englishman John Nelson Darby (1800-1882), Independent Fundamental churches distinguish themselves from Baptists by their belief in dispensationalism. The Fundamentalists believe the Bible is a history of God's actions with people in different periods: the church, now in ruins, representing one such dispensation. Another distinguishing feature is the belief that Christian assemblies are a unity of the Spirit, and not of organization. The Fundamentalist family frequently uses the *Scofield Reference Bible* as a major source for doctrine.

COMMUNAL FAMILY

Citing references to the early Christian church, members of the communal churches desire to share all their worldly possessions with other members of the group. Communalism may be identified with the monastic movement of the 4th century and onwards, which thought the principle of equality could be achieved through poverty and renunciation of the world.

Overleaf:
Baptism, China;
Episcopalian
chapel USA; The
Kingdom Choir in
concert; Russian
Orthodox
steeples,
Moscow; River
baptism, Africa;
Mennonite
chapel, USA;
Sacre Coeur,
Paris.

.2 Modern Groups

When the history of Christian growth in the 20th century has been looked at in historical perspective, the growth of the Pentecostal churches may be seen as one of the century's most important movements.

In the 20th century the Pentecostal Church has been the fastest-growing Church in South America. Between 1960 and 1980 it grew by over 500% over two-thirds of South America. Largely as a result of the expansion of Pentecostal churches, at the turn of the millennium there were more Christians per head of population in South America than anywhere else in the world.

HISTORY OF PENTECOSTALISM

Pentecostalism is a relatively modern branch of Christianity, growing out of the holiness movement, which in turn had roots in Methodism.

During the last two decades of the 19th century, there were reports of xenoglossia (the speaking of a foreign language by a person who has no familiarity with it) breaking out at revival meetings, particularly in North and South Carolina. There may also have been some instances of glossolalia (ecstatic speech).

In 1899 a great rise in religious fervor grew as people speculated about the second coming of Jesus and the end of history as they knew it. On January 1, 1900, Charles F. Parham, a holiness preacher and head of the Bethel Bible College in Topeka, Kansas, conducted a revival meeting in that city at which Agnes Ozman, a Methodist, shocked the meeting by speaking fluently in a number of foreign languages that she had never learned. This event is often regarded as the founding of the Pentecostal movement. Some days later, many spoke in tongues, including Parham.

Until 1914, the movement worked primarily within the holiness churches. But increasing friction motivated the

Fervent prayer is a mark of modern Pentecostalism.

Pentecostal meeting, USA.

Pentecostals to form their first denomination, the Assemblies of God.

✛ THREE EXPERIENCES

Some Pentecostals, particularly those with a holiness background, believe in the 'Pentecostal experience' as the third of three experiences:

1. Justification (faith and trust by the believer in Jesus as Lord and Savior),
2. sanctification (the 'second blessing' – the imparting of new life to the believer by the Holy Spirit),
3. baptism of the Holy Spirit (as evidenced by speaking in tongues).

✛ PENTECOSTAL DENOMINATIONS

Two of the main Pentecostal denominations are the Church of God (Cleveland TN), and the Church of God in Christ.

✛ ONENESS PENTECOSTALS

Oneness Pentecostals (also known as 'Jesus Only' or 'Apostolic Pentecostals') accept the 'oneness' of God and do not believe in the Trinity. The United Pentecostal Church and the Pentecostal Assemblies of the World are the main Oneness Pentecostal denominations. They have over 2.3 million members worldwide, including about 600,000 members in their 3,764 North American churches.

Oral Roberts, controversial charismatic preacher.

BAPTIST BIBLE FELLOWSHIP INTERNATIONAL

In 1909, in response to attacks on historic Christianity by liberal German theologians, a five-volume work called *The Fundamentals* was published. The following 14 fundamentals, considered essential to Christianity, were presented:

1.	The inspiration of the Bible
2.	The depravity of man
3.	Redemption through Christ's blood
4.	The true church made up only of believers
5.	The coming of the Lord bodily to set up his reign
6.	The Trinity
7.	The fall of Adam
8.	The need of the new birth
9.	Full deliverance from guilt at salvation
10.	The assurance of salvation
11.	The centrality of Christ in the Bible
12.	The walk after the Spirit
13.	The resurrection of both believers and unbelievers
14.	The ripening of the present age for judgment

In 1921, in the United States, fundamentalists such as W. B. Riley, J. Frank Norris, and T. T. Shields organized the Baptist Bible Union to voice their united stand for the fundamentals in opposition to modernism.

In 1928 the World Fundamental Baptist Missionary Fellowship (later shortened to World Baptist Fellowship) was established under the leadership of Norris as a reaction against modernist inroads in the Southern Baptist Convention.

In 1932 the General Association of Regular Baptist Churches was established under the leadership of Robert Ketcham as a reaction against liberalism in the Northern Baptist Convention. Difficulties from within the former group brought the BBFI into existence.

✛ THE BBFI IN THE 1990s

The work of the BBFI – soul winning, church planting, world missions, church building, touching and discipling lives – remains the purpose of the Fellowship. Over 3,300 pastors and churches who identify with this movement are listed in the Fellowship Directory. More than 800 BBFI missionaries are serving on 95 fields of the world.

THE CHURCH OF GOD OF PROPHECY

The Church of God of Prophecy traces its founding back to the teaching of Mark 3:13-19 in the New Testament when Jesus commissioned his 12 apostles. Radical reform groups of the 16th century, such as Anabaptists, Mennonites, Baptists, and

Quakers, contended that the major reformers had fallen short of a complete restoration of God's church. The radical reformers, therefore, sought to restore the church on the basis of deep spiritual experiences, personal piety, and strict moral discipline.

When groups of radical reformers emigrated to America in the 16th and 17th centuries, their ideas flourished. In America, and elsewhere, they emphasized experiential salvation, God's love, and practical holiness. Great revivals, some marked by Pentecostal manifestations, occurred among the radical reform groups, especially the Baptists and the followers of George Whitefield and John Wesley. Following in this tradition, the forefathers of the Church of God of Prophecy viewed their work as both a continuation and restoration of the apostolic church.

Under the leadership of Milton Tomlinson, the Church expanded into every state in America and to more than 90 countries worldwide.

THE CHURCH OF THE NAZARENE

Organized on October 8, 1908, in Pilot Point, Texas, the Church of the Nazarene has been based in Kansas City since shortly after the birth of the denomination.

The Nazarene International Center provides support services to more than 1.2 million members worshiping in more than 11,800 churches in the United States, Canada, and 114 other world areas. Services include maintaining ministerial credentials and church records, coordinating the support and sending of missionaries, developing Sunday school and discipleship curriculum, providing retirement support programs for pastors, encouraging the starting of new churches, developing satellite, internet, and radio programs for outreach and education to all parts of the globe, and much more.

✠ PUBLISHING

The Nazarene Publishing House (NPH) is the largest publisher of holiness (Wesleyan) literature in the world. NPH prints more than 500,000 books annually.

✠ WORLD OUTREACH

Nazarenes have 665 missionaries and volunteers serving in 116 areas around the world.

✠ THEOLOGY

The Church of the Nazarene is the largest denomination in the Wesleyan-Arminian theological tradition. The doctrine that distinguishes the Church of the Nazarene and other Wesleyan denominations from most other Christian denominations is 'entire sanctification.' Nazarenes believe that God calls Christians to a life of holy living that is marked by an act of God in which the heart is cleansed from original sin and the individual is filled with love for God and humankind. This experience is marked by entire consecration of the believer to do God's will and is followed by a life of seeking to serve God through service to others.

THE EVANGELICAL LUTHERAN CHURCH IN AMERICA (ELCA)

The Evangelical Lutheran Church in America resulted from the union, in 1982,

QUICK FACTS ABOUT THE CHURCH OF THE NAZARENE

Current membership worldwide	1,254,315
New Nazarenes in 1997	85,292
Number of organized churches	12,134
Number of districts	363
Ordained elders	12,547
NWMS (Nazarene World Mission Society) membership	698,145
NYI (Nazarene Youth International) membership	307,563
Total giving for all purposes	$586,908,906

Figures from 1997

QUICK FACTS ABOUT THE ELCA

Baptized members	5,178,255
Communing and contributing members	2,501,669
Included are	
African-Americans	50,635
Hispanics	32,295
Asians and Pacific Islanders	22,467
Average worship attendance each week	1,579,871
Congregations	10,862
Clergy	17,681
Female	2,296
People of color	427
Missionaries	310
Average annual giving per confirmed member	$447.89

Figures from 1999

of three North American Lutheran Churches: the American Lutheran Church, the Association of Evangelical Lutheran Churches and the Lutheran Church in America.

LUTHERAN WORLD FEDERATION

Zhenjiang Gospel Church, China.

The Lutheran World Federation (LWF) is a global communion of Lutheran churches. Founded in 1947, by 1999 it had 128 member churches in 70 countries representing 58 million of the world's 61.5 million Lutherans.

The LWF acts on behalf of its member churches in areas of common interest such as ecumenical relations, theology, humanitarian assistance, human rights, communication, and the various aspects of mission and development work.

HOUSE-CHURCH MOVEMENT

Since the mid 1960s disillusioned Christians have left the institutional church by the thousands.

✣ 'SECOND REFORMATION'

There is a growing realization that our present church structures are inadequate to meet the demands of a changing society. Many people doubt whether existing churches are flexible enough to cope with a major outpouring of the Spirit of God. Ralph Neighbour, a pioneer and proponent of cell group churches, has called for a 'second Reformation.' He suggests that present church structures are woefully inadequate.

✣ BRIDGE BUILDERS

Ralph Neighbour suggests that in the church we need bridge builders: people willing to work toward new models of church life and ministry. House churches are bridges. They are the most appropriate context for the expression of Christian community.

'On biblical and contemporary grounds the Home Church is fundamental to any quest for renewal.' ROBERT BANK

✣ HOUSE CHURCHES IN CHINA

Ross Paterson, commenting on Chinese house churches, writes: 'Churches which lost their buildings and their corporate life (after the cultural revolution) became centered around and rooted in the family, as meetings had to be held in homes. This lack of structure has proved of enormous benefit to the church in China.'

House group
Bible study.

'Church buildings are not made for fellowship but homes are. And it was in homes that early Christians met to worship.'
RON SNYDER

✤ WORLDWIDE MOVEMENT
The concept of the church in the house is not a new one. Throughout the history of the Christian church there is evidence of God's people meeting in homes. This is illustrated by the Basic Christian Communities in Central America, the revival taking place in Communist China, the growth of Icthus fellowship in London, Faith Community Baptist Church in Singapore, and the number of independent house churches that have begun worldwide.

✤ A PROFILE OF HOUSE CHURCHES
- House churches are not seen as an extra on top of the real thing, that is, church on Sunday. On the contrary, the house church is the church; the nucleus of the church's life and ministry.
- House churches are networked together in a 'pastorate system.' The house church is the church, but the house churches also meet together at times for a Celebration Service in a rented hall.
- Each is led by an unpaid pastor. These pastors meet regularly with the pastorate leaders for training and encouragement.

Members of this movement believe that if the basic unit of the Christian community became the church in the home, then many more people could be reached with the good news of Jesus.

SOUTHERN BAPTISTS

✤ BAPTIST FAITH AND MESSAGE
Since its organization in 1845 in Augusta, Georgia, the Southern Baptist Convention (SBC) has grown to 15.8 million members who worship in more than 40,000 churches in the United States. Southern Baptists sponsor about 5,000 home missionaries serving the United States, Canada, and the Caribbean, as well as sponsoring more than 4,000 foreign missionaries in 126 nations of the world.

The term Southern Baptist Convention denotes both the denomination and its annual meeting. Working through 1,221 local associations and 39 state conventions and fellowships, Southern Baptists share a common bond of basic biblical beliefs and a commitment to proclaim the gospel of Jesus Christ to the entire world.

The Convention's purpose, as stated in Article II of its constitution, is 'to provide a general organization for Baptists in the United States and its territories for the promotion of Christian missions at home and abroad.'

In 1996, Southern Baptist churches gave more that $274 million through the Cooperative Program and special foreign and home missions offerings.

CARRYING THE CROSS

'Carrying the cross is simply a reminder of Jesus' death and resurrection,' explains Keith Wheller. Keith began carrying a 12-foot wooden cross on Good Friday, 1985, in obedience to God's call. He has now carried the cross over 11,500 miles, through more than 75 countries. He has been arrested many times, beaten and left for dead, and even taken before a firing squad to be shot.

JOINING HANDS ACROSS THE NATIONS –
MARCHES FOR JESUS THROUGHOUT THE WORLD

1987 *Ichthus Fellowship* in London joined with *Youth With A Mission* and *Pioneer Team* to organize a prayer and praise march through the streets of London. More than 15,000 people joined in.

1988 The marches attracted 55,000 people throughout England.

1989 Tom and Theresa Pelton of Austin, Texas, attended a worship leaders' conference in California where Graham Kendrick presented the march vision. Pelton then organized the first city-wide march, in which 1,500 Christians took part.

1990 15,000 Christians marched in Austin's second praise march.

1992 300,000 Christians in 142 US cities and 300,000 Christians in 25 European countries marched for Jesus. 500 believers marched through Moscow's Gorky Park.

1993 brought 1.7 million Christians to the streets in 850 cities across the globe. In the US, about 800,000 believers marched for Jesus through the streets of 350 US cities.

1994 1.5 million believers across America from 550 cities joined in the March for Jesus. All around the world 10 million people marched in more than a thousand cities in 178 nations.

1995 2,190 towns around the world joined in the March for Jesus, including one million Christians in the USA.

1996 11 million joined in the *March for Jesus,* with 1 million from the USA. In Japan, 4,000 people marched in 29 cities.

1997 more than 6 million people worldwide marched simply because they love Jesus. In the United States, an estimated 1 million people marched in more than 700 cities in all 50 states.

1998 700,000 people in 633 cities in the United States and more than 10 million people worldwide took to the streets to worship Jesus. Around the world prayers were offered up for those who are persecuted and suffer because of their Christian faith.

Since 1987, the world has witnessed over 45 million people marching for Jesus.

March for Jesus rally, Trafalgar Square, London.

✣ MARCHING FOR GOD
March led by the Salvation Army and Methodists

In l885, the Salvation Army marched to the British Houses of Parliament with a petition of 343,000 signatures, demanding that the trade in child prostitution be stopped and the age of consent be raised from 13 to 16 years old. The law was changed as a result of such marches.

Why march?

March for Jesus is a national and international event that unites churches of all denominations in cities across the world to share their common faith in Jesus Christ. Taking the church to the streets breaks down barriers between churches and leads to greater unity and cooperation.

What happens at a *March for Jesus?*

In an atmosphere much like a family gathering, believers of all ages come together to march down their city streets. During the actual March, mobile sound units play lively music, written specifically for the March. As they sing songs, recite proclamations and wave colorful banners, participants show their love for God. The March concludes with a prayer rally for the city, nation and world led by local pastors.

Celebration

The annual event is a worldwide celebration of Jesus Christ. Participants march together and sing the March music, which contains upbeat choruses, proclamations, and well-known hymns.

Prayer

At the Prayer Rally for the March, Christians join hands and hearts as they pray for their city and their nation. Believers ask for God's wisdom and blessing on their local government officials.

Unity

Christians set their denominational differences aside to come together for this unifying event. They show that there is actually only one church in the city, with many congregations. *March for Jesus* is a reunion of the entire church in the city, celebrated by followers of Jesus from every background and race.

World's largest *March for Jesus*

The world's largest *March for Jesus* took place in Sao Paulo, Brazil, where 300,000 Christians marched.

PROMISE KEEPERS

Promise Keepers is a Christian outreach aimed at building men of integrity. Through stadium conferences, ongoing local small groups, educational seminars, resource materials, and local churches, *Promise Keepers* encourages men to live godly lives and to keep their basic promises of commitment to God, their families, and fellow men.

✣ BEGINNINGS

On March 20, 1990, the head football coach for the University of Colorado, Bill McCartney, and his friend Dave Wardell PhD, were on a three-hour car ride to a *Fellowship of Christian Athletes* (FCA) meeting, when they first discussed the idea of filling a stadium with Christian men. Later that year, 72 men began to fast and pray about the concept of thousands of men coming together for the purpose of Christian discipleship. In July 1991, 4,200 men gathered for the first *Promise Keepers* conference at the University of Colorado basketball arena. Since then, more than 3.2 million men have attended 83 *Promise Keepers* stadium and arena conferences.

5.3 MISSION GROUPS

Christian mission groups are often more in step with each other than many of the large Christian denominations. A massive organization like *Fire of Life Youth Ministry*, which claims to be the largest youth ministry in the US, and a more modest mission like *Christian Outreach International*, which focuses evangelism among baseball players and coaches, have identical aims: to bring the good news about Jesus to people in a relevant way. Jerry Kindall, Head Baseball Coach, University of Arizona, captured the spirit of evangelism when he said: 'By going out on a mission trip with *Christian Outreach International*, player or coach has an incredible opportunity to see God work in and through their lives in ways they may never experience otherwise. Such a trip is a great way to help fulfill the Great Commission.'

ICHTHUS INTERNATIONAL

Ichthus is a non-profit-making, international Christian organization of youth clubs. *Ichthus* consists of thousands of volunteers working with 15,000 children and teenagers throughout Latin America and in the US, providing Bible study, discipleship, fellowship, and leadership training.

A low-cost program was developed, 30 years ago, in Guatemala, called Ichthus – the Greek word for fish and a symbol for early Christians in Roman times. *Ichthus* provides nurture, personal development, Christian growth, and leadership training through fun-filled meetings and activities such as camping.

JEWS FOR JESUS

'We exist to make the Messiahship of Jesus an unavoidable issue to our Jewish people worldwide. Our message is that Jesus (in Hebrew, Y'shua) is the Messiah promised to the Jewish people and the Savior of the world; that he accomplished our salvation by dying as an atonement for our sins and rising again on the third day; and that anyone, Jew or Gentile, who believes in him will be saved.'
MOISHE ROSEN, FOUNDER, *JEWS FOR JESUS*

THE MESSIANIC JEWISH ALLIANCE OF AMERICA

The Messianic Jewish Alliance of America is the largest association of Messianic Jewish believers in Yeshua (Jesus) in the world. Established in 1915, the specific and special ministry of the *MJAA* is threefold:
1. To promote a clear and visible testimony to the fact that there is a large and growing movement of Jewish people who believe that Yeshua is the Jewish Messiah and Savior of the world,

2. to bring together, in one organization, Jewish and non-Jewish people, of like faith and mind, with a shared vision for Jewish revival,
3. to introduce our Jewish brothers and sisters to the Messiah Yeshua.

The *MJAA* is affiliated with Messianic Jewish Alliances in 15 other countries, including Israel.

YOUTH WITH A MISSION

YWAM is one of the world's largest missionary groups. 16% of the mission's worldwide staff are living and working in the regions of the globe home to most of the world's unreached people groups. *YWAM* has 630 ministry centers around the world with a total staff of 10,622.

✢ KING'S KIDS

King's Kids International is a worldwide youth ministry committed to leading children and teens of all nations into a proven knowledge of God and to making Jesus Christ known to all peoples in the fulfilling of the Great Commission.

King's Kids equips, challenges, mobilizes, and establishes this 'emerging generation' of young people through a partnership with the family, the local church, and *YWAM*. Its motto is: Training tomorrow's leaders ... today!

'The demands of modern education keep young people from the dignity of hands-on work in the market place but youth should not be kept from ministering to the world. *King's Kids'* programs employ the youngest Christians in the challenging work of intercession and evangelization, and it works.'
JOHN DAWSON

THE BOYS' BRIGADE

The Boys' Brigade, the oldest uniformed youth organization in the world, has an anchor as its emblem and 'Sure and Steadfast' as its motto, words taken from Hebrews 6:19. *The Boy's Brigade* was founded on October 4, 1883, by William Alexander Smith at the Free College Church Mission, North Woodside Road, Glasgow, Scotland. A Sunday school teacher, Smith devised a unique system of giving boys an organization, as part of the church, based on religion and discipline.

His object was: 'The advancement of Christ's kingdom among boys and the promotion of habits of obedience, reverence, discipline, self-respect and all that tends towards a true Christian manliness.' This is achieved by delivering Christian teaching in partnership with the church in which the company is based and encouraging the development of a personal Christian faith.

US CENTER FOR WORLD MISSION

The US Center for World Mission (*USCWM*) is a non-profit-making, interdenominational Christian organization dedicated to furthering the great commission throughout the earth. The primary focus of the Center is to promote Christian mission mobilization activities so that all peoples of the world may have the opportunity to hear the gospel of the Lord Jesus Christ.

The *USCWM* is a 35-acre complex dedicated to the promotion of US and global efforts to reach the world's remaining mission fields – 10,000 unreached people groups (2.1 billion people). Almost 50

agencies have offices in the complex and share the *USCWM*'s facilities for training, meetings, and strategic planning sessions.

CHRISTIAN MISSION FOR THE DEAF (CMD)

'Approximately 1 out of every 1,000 persons is deaf or suffers from impaired hearing.

'Meeting the human needs of the deaf requires special skills and services. It is the goal of *CMD* to reach the educational and spiritual needs of those who face these challenges.'

DR ANDREW FOSTER

CMD is a non-profit-making organization specializing in reaching deaf Africans with the gospel message through schools and Sunday schools. Since its founding in 1957, *CMD*'s objectives have been to organize, operate, maintain, promote and encourage gospel and education work among the deaf of Africa, working in over 30 countries. Training local African Christian workers and leaders has been an instrumental method of its outreach.

LUIS PALAU

The *Wall Street Journal* of November 1995 called Luis Palau 'The Billy Graham of everywhere.' During more than 30 years of mass evangelism, evangelist Luis Palau has spoken to hundreds of millions of people in 104 nations through radio and television broadcasts, and face-to-face to 13 million people in 68 nations. Since 1990, the *Luis Palau Evangelistic Association* has led evangelistic crusades in 20 US cities, including Chicago, Kansas City, Grand Rapids, Miami, Tulsa, San Antonio, Phoenix, Fort Worth, and the San Fernando Valley in Los Angeles.

More than half a million people have committed their lives to Jesus Christ through Palau evangelistic meetings.

'I wholeheartedly believe in one-on-one evangelism,' says Dr Palau. 'But it can only be a complement to the greater movement

Luis Palau, South American evangelist.

of God within a nation. You can prepare the groundwork, but eventually it's necessary to move the masses and sway public opinion. A nation will not be changed by timid methods.'

CAMPUS CRUSADE

Campus Crusade for Christ is an interdenominational ministry committed to helping take the gospel of Jesus Christ to all nations. It cooperates with millions of Christians from churches of many denominations and hundreds of other Christian organizations around the world to help Christians grow in their faith and share the gospel message with their fellow countrymen.

Campus Crusade for Christ International states that its aims are:

- equipping parents, teachers, administrators, and coaches to reach high school students for Christ and assist their growth in faith,
- helping college students, volunteers,

faculty members and local churches launch and grow new universities and college campus ministries,

- providing coaching, training and resources; equipping those who desire to start a ministry to college athletes,
- providing coaching, training and resources to key professionals who want to reach out to the executive professional ministry,
- providing resources to families of inmates, youth at risk, victims of crime, law enforcement and correction officers, or prison inmates,
- equipping men and women in the armed forces to face personal and professional challenges, opportunities, and uncertainties unparalleled in civilian life with proven resources and expert coaching,
- equipping parents with proven resources to more effectively build a strong marriage and family relationships.

CHURCH ARMY USA

The Church Army is a society of trained and commissioned evangelists in the Episcopal Church who minister the gospel of Jesus Christ in word and deed especially among the most needy and socially marginalized people.

The Church Army was born in 1882 out of a movement of revival which flowed from the great Prayer Revival of 1858. This remarkable lay movement produced a great outpouring of zeal for mission both at home and in foreign mission fields. Earnest souls experienced a baptism of fire which inspired them to go out in faith and to give costly service in the hardest and most difficult places.

When the streets of London filled with unemployed workers following the financial collapse of 1873, these fiery Christians took to the streets to bring the love of Jesus to desperate and forgotten people. They preached that ordinary men and women could experience pardon, purity, and power through the saving work of Jesus on the cross and his outpoured Spirit. Churches formed 'gospel armies' to carry on this work. In 1882 Wilson Carlile banded together several gospel armies to form the *Church Army of the Church of England.*

✤ CALLED TO AMERICA

By the 1930s the movement had spread to the Commonwealth countries and to the United States. The first contingent of 24 English officers came to the United States in 1925 and conducted an evangelistic tour through New York City and New England to Canada, preaching at open air stations and churches along the way. In 1926 Carlile went to the US at the urgent invitation of Bishop Manning and several other bishops who had heard of the effectiveness of Church Army's lay evangelists. A group of trained Church Army captains accompanied Carlile and stayed to participate in the Bishops' Crusade, a nation-wide evangelistic effort launched by the House of Bishops in 1927. Carlile also met with Sam Shoemaker and one of the early marches started from the steps of Pittsburgh's Trinity Cathedral.

5.4 RELIEF ORGANIZATIONS

From the most cursory reading of Paul's letters and James' letter in the New Testament it is clear that all Christians should be engaged in good deeds. However, many theologians have argued that James and Paul contradict each other on this matter and cause confusion about this subject. In a similar way, in the 1960s, many Christians were suspicious of the prominence given to social action. Today, most Christians agree that preaching the gospel and attending to humanitarian needs go hand in hand.

SALVATION ARMY

The objectives of the *Salvation Army* are 'the advancement of the Christian religion, of education, the relief of poverty, and other charitable objects beneficial to society or the community of mankind as a whole.'

The movement, founded in 1865 by William Booth, has spread from London, England, to many parts of the world. Its evangelistic and social enterprises are maintained under the authority of the General by full-time officers, employees, and soldiers who give service in their free time.

Evengeline Booth (1865-1950) became the first woman commander of any Salvation Army branch when she became commander of the US branch in 1904. She was commander for 30 years.

Internationally, the *Salvation Army* works in just over 100 countries using more than 140 languages. There are over 14,000 Corps (centers for worship) as well as a wide range of social, medical, educational and other community services.

The Family Tracing Service was established in 1885 for the purpose of trying to restore (or to sustain) family relationships, by locating relatives who for whatever reason have lost contact.

TEARFUND (THE EVANGELICAL ALLIANCE RELIEF FUND)

Tearfund was founded in 1968 by the *Evangelical Alliance* as a relief and development agency. It is a separate independent organization with its own Board and membership. In 2001 it employed over 200 staff in Britain, with a similar number of overseas specialist workers.

Its aims are to bring physical and spiritual help as an expression of Christian responsibility to those in need in developing countries. *Tearfund* finances development

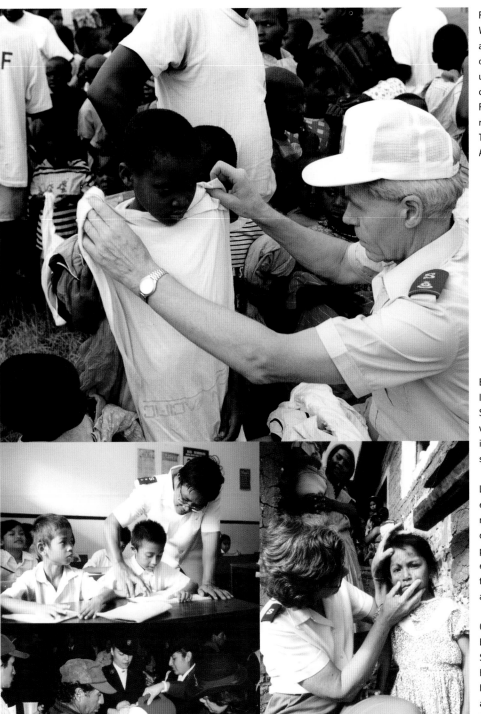

Rwandan Civil War 1994: a Salvation Army officer measures up a child for clothing in a Rwandan refugee camp, Tanzania, east Africa.

Bandung, Indonesia: Salvationist visitor assists in a primary school.

Lima, Peru: each night corps members hand out rolls and pink (vitamin-enriched) milk to the homeless and destitute.

Cochacamba, Bolivia: Salvationist health projects help fight against parasite infestation that shortens the life expectancy of this girl to about 25 years.

A smiling child in Sudan.

A little boy pumps water in India from a newly-supplied well from a Tearfund program.

Mother and baby in Cochabamba, Bolivia, supported by the Tearfund health program.

Tearfund enables the management of fish-farming in north-east Thailand.

and emergency relief projects initiated and implemented by expatriates and nationals, and supports personnel to work in developing countries. It produces educational and promotional materials for British Christians and an annual Tearcraft catalogue of fairly-traded products.

TRAIDCRAFT

Traidcraft is the UK's largest independent fair trade organization, selling over £3 million of goods in the UK in 1998. At first *Traidcraft* sold teas, coffee and some dried fruit and nuts but their extended range of high-quality breakfast mueslis, chocolate bars and snack products are proving increasingly popular with consumers – and that is making a real difference in the 'third world.'

Traidcraft is a co-founder of *Cafédirect* and attributes part of its sales growth to this dynamic coffee brand.

Traidcraft's best-selling textile product is a block-printed unbleached duvet set from Aarong, a Bangladesh marketing organization run to help rural craft workers, mostly women.

MOTHER TERESA OF CALCUTTA AND THE MISSIONARIES OF CHARITY

Agnes Gonxha Bojaxhiu (1910-1997), an Albanian-born Roman Catholic nun, was deeply moved by the presence of the sick and dying on the city streets of Calcutta.

In 1948 she began a ministry among the sick. In 1950 Mother Teresa and her associates were approved within the archdiocese of Calcutta as the *Missionaries of Charity*. Later the order was recognized as a pontifical congregation under the jurisdiction of Rome.

Members of the congregation take four vows on acceptance by the religious community. Required in addition to the three basic vows of poverty, chastity, and obedience is a fourth vow pledging service to the poor, whom Mother Teresa described as the embodiment of Christ. In 1952 Mother Teresa opened the Nirmal Hriday ('Pure Heart') Home for Dying Destitutes in Calcutta. Subsequently she extended her work on to five continents. In recognition of her efforts she was awarded the Nobel Peace Prize in 1979.

5.5 SERVICE GROUPS

When the first apostles became inundated with administrative work they appointed seven men, such as Stephen, to relieve them of this work so that they did not 'neglect the ministry of the word of God in order to wait on tables' (Acts 6:2). These seven Christians, who could be called the first Christian service agency, were 'full of the Spirit and wisdom' (Acts 6:3). Christians who work in Christian service organizations are following in their footsteps. In Acts we are told: 'The word of God spread. The number of disciples ... increased rapidly' (Acts 6:7).

GOSPEL COMMUNICATIONS NETWORK

In 1994, conversations between *Gospel Films* Director of Marketing Duane Smith and *Calvin College* Communications Professor Quentin Schultze, gave birth to an idea for spreading the gospel on the Internet.

The idea was presented to *Gospel Films* President Billy Zeoli, who quickly caught the vision and had the team present the plan to the *Gospel Films* Board of Directors. The Board, under the chairmanship of Richard M. DeVos, also saw the great potential for ministry in this new medium.

Under Zeoli's leadership, the plan now included inviting other Christian ministries to join in an online alliance to:

* promote cooperation among likeminded organizations;
* minimize duplication of efforts; and
* maximize online traffic.

The GCI-sponsored alliance was to be called the *Gospel Communications Network*.

In April 1995 *Gospelcom* went online with ten ministry organizations.

✠ MISSION STATEMENT

'Being convinced that the responsibility for evangelizing the world with the gospel of Jesus Christ is the imperative task of dedicated Christians and that the Internet technology offers an effective vehicle in the accomplishment of this task, we propose to operate the *Gospel Communications Network* as an alliance of online Christian ministries.'

CHRISTIAN AID

The primary purpose of *Christian Aid* (not to be confused with a relief organization with the same name) is to encourage and strengthen New Testament Christianity,

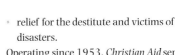

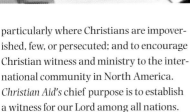

particularly where Christians are impoverished, few, or persecuted; and to encourage Christian witness and ministry to the international community in North America. *Christian Aid's* chief purpose is to establish a witness for our Lord among all nations.

✠ MISSIONARY WORK

Christian Aid collects funds from missionary-minded Christians here and sends them to indigenous mission agencies in poor countries. These indigenous groups send out missionaries to their own people.

Christian Aid Mission is in touch with hundreds of indigenous Christian mission agencies in poor and oppressed lands, especially in lands where evangelism is greatly needed. *Christian Aid* supports only those ministries which hold to the fundamental doctrines of historic evangelical Christianity.

✠ HOW THE GIFT MONEY IS USED

- Planting churches,
- evangelizing the unreached,
- training and sending out missionaries,
- discipling believers,
- operating schools and training institutes,
- caring for needy children and widows,
- medical clinics and literacy programs,
- translating and publishing Bibles and Christian literature,
- producing evangelistic films and videos,

- relief for the destitute and victims of disasters.

Operating since 1953, *Christian Aid* sends help to over 400 such ministries which have more than 30,000 missionaries on the field.

BIBLE COLLEGES

The *London Bible College*, based in Northwood, 15 miles outside London, is the largest inter-denominational theological college in Western Europe.

✠ VISION COLLEGES

Vision Colleges are specialist Bible colleges. They provide ministerial, theological, biblical and Christian studies through distance learning (correspondence courses) to students who are unable to attend a Bible college.

They now have an Internet Bible college, bringing their courses to places that were previously out of reach,

They also specialize in setting up and supporting local, Church-based Bible colleges, called 'Satellite colleges' and have 1,000 Satellites in over 98 countries, helping over 30,000 students.

Bible college students at work and relaxing.

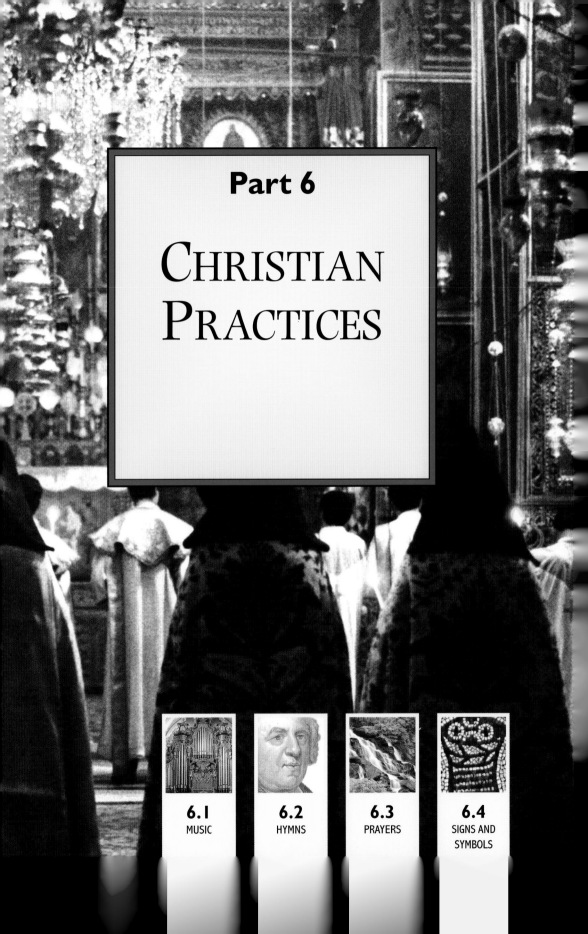

Part 6

CHRISTIAN PRACTICES

6.1
MUSIC

6.2
HYMNS

6.3
PRAYERS

6.4
SIGNS AND
SYMBOLS

6.1 MUSIC

Music has always been greatly appreciated by God's people. Music was used in worship in the Old Testament, as many of the psalms indicate. William Booth used tambourines in his worship and said: 'Music is for the soul what wind is for the ship, blowing her onwards in the direction in which she is steered.'

✠ MUSIC DESERVES THE HIGHEST PRAISE

Singing was always an important part of Martin Luther's life. As a young student, he earned money to pay his college fees by singing in the streets of Eisenach.

Luther, who also played the flute, wrote: 'Next to the Word of God, music deserves the highest praise. She is a mistress and governess of those human emotions ... which control men or more often overwhelm them. Whether you wish to comfort the sad, to subdue frivolity, to encourage the despairing, to humble the proud, to calm the passionate, or to appease those full of hate ... what more effective means than music could you find?'

✠ LASTING ROYAL EXAMPLE

When *Messiah* was performed before King George II of England in 1743, the king rose as the triumphal notes of the Hallelujah Chorus were first played. Of course, everyone had to rise when the king did, and so began the tradition of rising for the Hallelujah Chorus – a tradition that continues to this day.

The main organ pipes: part of the vast organ at Passau Cathedral.

ORGANS

✠ LARGEST CHURCH ORGAN

The world's largest organ, built in 1928 by D. F. Steinmeyer & Co, is in Passau Cathedral, Germany. It has five manuals and 16,000 pipes.

✠ GREATEST NUMBER OF PIPES

The organ with the greatest number of pipes, 18,200, is in the chapel at West Point US Military Academy, New York.

✠ BRITAIN'S LARGEST ORGAN

The Anglican Cathedral in Liverpool has Britain's largest organ, with 9,704 pipes.

J.S. BACH

THE FIFTH EVANGELIST

The famous missionary doctor Albert Schweitzer, a highly accomplished organist and expert on Bach, gave him the title of 'the Fifth Evangelist.'

For a three-year period Bach composed a new cantata for every Sunday of the year. Each week this involved copying out the music for the singers and players, and rehearsing them, as well as the actual composing of the music. Bach, a devout Lutheran, is most remembered for his *St Matthew Passion*, which he composed in 1727.

J.S. Bach.

MOST WIDELY RECORDED COMPOSER

There are more recordings of Bach's music than that of any other composer.

MUSICAL INSTRUMENTS IN THE BIBLE

Music-makers were important people in Bible times. On all important occasions – happy and sad – people turned to music. The Psalms comprised the hymn book of the Israelites. Women were not allowed to play music in the Temple, but specially-trained priests accompanied the singing on timbrels, trumpets, horns, pipes, large lyres, sistrums, cymbals (loud cymbals and high sounding cymbals), lutes and flutes.

PRAISING GOD WITH SONG

Why do we clap our hands and have audible praise to God?

'Clap your hands, all you nations; shout to God with cries of joy.'
PSALM 47:1

'Shout for joy to the LORD, all the earth, burst into jubilant song with music; make music to the LORD with the harp, with the harp and the sound of singing, with trumpets and the blast of the ram's horn – shout for joy before the LORD, the King.'
PSALM 98:4-6

GREGORIAN CHANT

In the Middle Ages church music was dominated by the type of music practiced in Rome. According to tradition, this dated back to Pope Gregory I. Numerous traditional melodies were organized until they were categorized into eight church modes. Each melody was given a specific place in the liturgical year, and some for different monastic services such as Matins, Vespers and Compline.

The Gregorian chant repertory expanded in the 9th century when the practice of troping originated. A trope is a text which is added to an existing melody. The added syllables made the long textless passages easier to remember. Tuotilo, who died in 915, a monk of St Gall in Switzerland, is credited with the invention of tropes.

Notker Balbulus introduced a long hymn as a trope to the final syllable of the Alleluia in the Eucharist.

TAIZÉ CHANTS

The Taizé Community is in a tiny village hidden away in the hills of Burgundy in the eastern part of France. It is an ecumenical community of brothers for whom prayer is at the heart of their life. Founded in 1940, the community is made up of Protestants and Catholics from 20 different countries, and has become host to thousands of young people who visit Taizé, entering into the prayer and spirit of the community. In reaching out to the greater body of God's people, the community has endeavored to make prayer meditative, popular, accessible to all generations, and as universal as possible. Simple chants, repeated over and over again, underscore the meditative quality of prayer. These are now known as 'Taizé' chants.

Overleaf: The All Souls Orchestra in concert.

6.2 HYMNS

One characteristic of a Christian, according to the apostle Paul, is that they 'sing psalms, hymns and spiritual songs' (Colossians 3:16).

Until the 18th-century evangelical revival, congregations sang stilted metrical versions of Scripture. Charles Wesley, 'the sweet singer of Methodism' composed a hymn practically every day, for 50 years, from the day of his conversion until the day of his death. It was through Charles Wesley that the doctrines of salvation, which his brother John preached, were sung by the thousands of new Christians in Great Britain and America. We still sing many of Charles Wesley's hymns, such as *Jesu, Lover of My Soul, Love Divine All Loves Excelling*, and *Hark the Herald Angels Sing*. The plaque on Charles Wesley's house in Bristol remains true: 'His hymns are the possession of the Christian Church.'

William Booth, founder of the *Salvation Army*, continued the tradition of exuberant music-making and hymn singing, saying, 'Why should the devil have all the best tunes?'

✠ FIRST CHRISTIAN HYMNS

Several of Paul's letters contain fragments of hymns from the first generation of Christians. The four most obvious are: Philippians 2:6-11; 1 Timothy 3:16; Ephesians 5:14; Colossians 1:15-20.

✠ FIRST ENGLISH HYMN BOOK

In the Church of England there were no hymn books in use for over 200 years after the Reformation. George Wither's *Hymnes and Songs of the Church*, published in 1623, was the first comprehensive English hymn book.

America's first 'hymn book' was *The Whole Book of Psalmes Faithfully Translated into English Metre*. It was published in 1640 and was the earliest book printed in English in America. This book was used by the Massachusetts Bay Colony and became known as *The Bay Psalm Book*.

✠ FIRST HYMN WRITTEN IN ENGLISH FOR PUBLIC WORSHIP

Behold the glories of the Lamb was written by Isaac Watts, in about 1688. This is the first hymn in the English language designed for public worship. In a lengthy discussion with his father, the young Watts argued that by singing only the Psalms in church Christians missed much important New Testament truth. Once his congregation was convinced of what Isaac was saying, he wrote a new hymn each week.

✠ OLDEST CHRISTIAN HYMN

Shepherd of tender youth (Shepherd of eager youth) was written by Clement of Alexandria, in about 200, and translated by Henry Martyn Dexter, in 1846. It is probably the oldest Christian hymn of which we know the author.

'Shepherd of tender youth, guiding in love and truth
Through devious ways; Christ our triumphant King,

We come Thy Name to sing and here our
children bring
To join Thy praise.'

✠ BATTLE HYMN OF THE REFORMATION

Luther wrote at least 37 hymns. His most
famous hymn, *A Mighty Fortress Is Our God*,
has been called the battle hymn of the
Reformation.

✠ HYMNS FROM THE PIETISTIC MOVEMENT

The 18th-century Pietist movement, with
its emphasis on what was called 'heart-reli-
gion' (*Herzensreligion*) was noted for its
hymn-writers. The hymns of Paul Gerhardt
(1606-76), Joachim Neander (1650-80)
and Gerhard Tersteegen (1697-1769) are
still sung and treasured by Christians today.

✠ *O SACRED HEAD, SORE WOUNDED*

'O sacred head, sore wounded,
Defiled and put to scorn;
O kingly head, surrounded
With mocking crown of thorn;
What sorrow mars thy grandeur?
Can death thy bloom deflower:
O countenance whose splendor
The hosts of heaven adore!'

P. GERHARDT

J. S. Bach adapted and harmonized a
melody of this hymn by H. L. Hassler and
included it in his *Passion According to St
Matthew*.

✠ DYING MAN'S HYMN

Abide with me was written by Henry Francis
Lyte in 1847.

Lyte was inspired to write this hymn as
he was dying of tuberculosis; he finished it
the Sunday he gave his farewell sermon to
his parish. The next day, he left for Italy to
try to regain his health, but he died in Nice,
France, three weeks after writing these
words. In his farewell sermon, he said, 'O
brethren, I stand here among you today, as
alive from the dead, if I may hope to
impress it upon you, and induce you to
prepare for that solemn hour which must
come to all, by a timely acquaintance with
the death of Christ.'

Every day the bells of his church at All
Saints in Lower Brixham, Devonshire, ring
out 'Abide with me.'

'Abide with me; fast falls the eventide;
The darkness deepens; Lord with me
abide.
When other helpers fail and comforts
flee,
Help of the helpless, O abide with me.'

John Newton,
the slave trader
who became a
hymn-writer.

✠ MOST POPULAR HYMN

Amazing Grace written by John Newton in
1779 is by far the most popular of our
hymns.

John Newton often composed a hymn to
fit in with the evening Bible readings. By
1779 he had written 280 hymns. They
were published with 68 hymns of Newton's
friend and parishioner, William Cowper, as
the *Olney Hymns*.

The hymn was inspired by David's words
recorded in 1 Chronicles 17:16-17, 'Then
King David went in and sat before the LORD,
and he said: "Who am I, O LORD God, and
what is my family, that you have brought
me this far? And as if this were not enough
in your sight, O God, you have spoken
about the future of the house of your
servant. You have looked on me as though I
were the most exalted of men, O LORD
God."'

✠ MOST PROLIFIC HYMN-WRITER

The most prolific hymn-writer is probably Frances Jane (Fanny) Crosby (1820-1915). She wrote over 8,000 hymns, using over 200 pseudonyms.

✠ OLDEST HYMN-WRITER

Fanny Crosby wrote her last hymn the day before her death at age 95.

✠ LONGEST HYMN

Bernard of Cluny's 2,966-line hymn, *Hora novissima tempora pessima sunt*, is the world's longest hymn.

✠ BLIND HYMN-WRITERS

Fanny Crosby, George Matheson, William Walford and Robert Williams were all blind.

✠ NOBEL PRIZE WINNING HYMN-WRITER

Rudyard Kipling was a hymn-writer who won a Nobel Prize. He won it for Literature in 1907.

✠ ROOSEVELT'S FAVORITE HYMN

Eternal Father, strong to save was written by William Whiting, 1860. He wrote the lyrics as a poem for a student about to sail for America. In America, *Eternal Father, strong to save* is often called the 'Navy Hymn' because it is sung at the Naval Academy in Annapolis, Maryland and on ships of the British Royal Navy. It was the favorite hymn of US President Franklin Roosevelt and was sung at his funeral in Hyde Park, New York, in April 1945. The Navy Band played it in 1963 as US President John Kennedy's body was carried up the steps of the US Capitol to lie in state.

✠ HYMN SUNG IN ACADEMY AWARD-WINNING MOVIE

Guide me, O thou great Jehovah (Guide me, O thou great Redeemer)
The words were written by William Williams, of Bristol, England in 1745. It was translated from Welsh to English by Peter Williams.

This hymn was sung, in Welsh, in the 1941 Academy Award winning movie *How Green Was My Valley*. It was also sung in English at the funeral of Diana, Princess of Wales, in Westminster Abbey, London, September 6, 1997.

O LITTLE TOWN OF BETHLEHEM

✠ CAROL INSPIRED BY THE CHURCH OF THE NATIVITY, BETHLEHEM

During a trip to the Holy Land in 1865, Philips Brooks was deeply moved as he was

✠ HYMN-WRITERS WELL KNOWN FOR THEIR SECULAR ACHIEVEMENTS

HYMN-WRITER	DATES	FAMED FOR BEING	WROTE THE HYMN
John Quincy Adams	1767-1848	American president	The Hour-Glass
Sarah Flower Adams	1805-1848	Actress, poet	Nearer, My God, to Thee
Sabine Baring-Gould	1834-1924	Writer	Onward, Christian Soldiers
William Blake	1757-1827	Poet	And Did Those Feet in Ancient Time
John Bowring	1792-1872	Diplomat, politician	In the Cross of Christ I Glory
John Bunyan	1628-1688	Author	He Who Would Valiant Be
John Byrom	1692-1763	Poet, diarist	Christians, Awake, Salute the Happy Morn
William Cowper	1731-1800	Poet	God Moves in a Mysterious Way
John Milton	1608-1674	Poet	Let Us with a Gladsome Mind
Christina Rossetti	1830-1894	Poet	In the Bleak Midwinter
Nahum Tate	1652-1715	Playwright, poet laureate	While Shepherds Watched Their Flocks
John Greenleaf Whittier	1807-1892	Poet	Dear Lord and Father of Mankind

Bethlehem at sunrise, with the Church of the Nativity silhouetted against the skyline.

worshiping in this church on Christmas Eve. Three years later Brooks wanted an outstanding carol for his children's Sunday School. He recalled his peaceful worship in the Church of the Nativity and wrote *O Little Town of Bethlehem*.

✤ CAROL COMMANDED TO BE SUNG EVERY CHRISTMAS EVE

Moisture from the Salzach River had caused the pipe organ of St Nicholas' Church, the Alpine village church of Oberndorf, Austria, to rust. Another tradition says that mice had gnawed holes in the bellows of the organ of St Nicholas' Church. On December 24, 1818, when Josef Mohr was told there could be no organ music for the Christmas Eve service, he wrote the words for *Stille Nacht! Heilige Nacht!, Silent Night, Holy Night*. He then asked the village organist, Franz Grüber, to compose a tune for this new carol, just in time for the choir to rehearse.

In 1834 *Silent Night* was performed for the king of Prussia. He then ordered that it should be sung every Christmas Eve by his cathedral choir.

FUNERALS

✤ GLADSTONE'S FUNERAL

Rock of Ages, cleft for me was written by Augustus Montague Toplady in 1776. There is a story that Toplady wrote it after taking shelter from a storm under a rocky overhang near England's Cheddar Gorge.

This hymn was sung at the funeral of William Gladstone in Westminster Abbey, London, England, as it was the politician's favorite hymn.

'Rock of Ages, cleft for me,
let me hide myself in Thee;
Let the water and the blood,
from Thy wounded side which flowed,
Be of sin the double cure;
save from wrath and make me pure.'

✤ CHURCHILL'S FUNERAL

O God, Our Help in Ages Past, written by Isaac Watts, was sung at the funeral of former British Prime Minister Winston Churchill in St Paul's Cathedral, London, 1965.

'O God, our Help in ages past,
Our Hope for years to come,
Our Shelter from the stormy blast,
And our eternal Home!'

Winston Churchill.

6.3 PRAYERS

Prayer has been part of the life of God's people since the time of Adam and Eve. The psalms consist of a wide variety of prayers, reflecting the many different moods and circumstances of the godly writers.

John the Baptist taught his followers about praying. When one of Jesus' disciples said to him, 'Lord, teach us to pray, just as John taught his disciples' (Luke 11:1), Jesus gave them the Lord's Prayer as a model to use.

✠ ONE OF THE EARLIEST EUROPEAN PRAYERS

The prayer called *St Patrick's Breastplate* is one of the earliest known European vernacular poems. While many scholars do not attribute it to Patrick, it certainly captures the spirit of Patrick's confession.

'I arise today
Through the mighty strength, the
    invocation of the Trinity.
Through belief in the threeness,
Through confession of the oneness
Of the Creator of Creation.

I arise today
Through the strength of Christ's birth
    with his baptism,
Through the strength of his crucifixion
    with his burial,
Through the strength of his resurrection
    with his ascension,
Through the strength of his descent for
    the judgment of Doom ...

Christ be with me, Christ within me,
Christ behind me, Christ before me,
Christ beside me, Christ to win me,
Christ to comfort and restore me,
Christ beneath me, Christ above me,
Christ in quiet, Christ in danger,
Christ in hearts of all that love me,
Christ in mouth of friend and stranger.'

PRAYERS OF THE FAMOUS

✠ ABRAHAM LINCOLN
'Lord, give us faith that right makes might.'

✠ MICHELANGELO
'Lord, make me see your glory in every place.'

✠ OLIVER CROMWELL
'Strengthen us, O God, to relieve the oppressed, to hear the groans of poor prisoners, to reform the abuses of all

Abraham Lincoln.

professions; that many be made not poor to make a few rich; for Jesus Christ's sake.

✣ R.L. STEVENSON
'Go with each of us to rest; if any awake, temper them the dark hours of watching; and when the day returns, return to us, our sun and comforter, and call us up with morning faces and with morning hearts, eager to labor, eager to be happy, if happiness should be our portion, and if the day be marked for sorrow, strong to endure it.'
(Written on the eve of his unexpected death.)

✣ SAMUEL JOHNSON
'Make me remember, O God, that every day is thy gift and ought to be used according to thy command, through Jesus Christ our Lord.'

✣ SIR FRANCIS DRAKE
'O Lord God, when thou givest to thy servants to endeavor any great matter, grant us also to know that it is not the beginning, but the continuing of the same to the end, until it be thoroughly finished, which yieldeth the true glory; through Him who for the finishing of Thy work laid down his life, our Redeemer, Jesus Christ. '
(Source unknown, based on a saying of Sir Francis Drake.

HMS *Victory*: Sir Francis Drake's ship.

✣ CHARLES KINGSLEY
'Take from us, O God, all pride and vanity, all boasting and self-assertiveness, and give us the true courage that shows itself by gentleness; the true wisdom that shows itself by simplicity; and the true power that shows itself by modesty; through Jesus Christ our Lord.'
(Author of *The Water Babies*.)

✣ KING HENRY VI
'O Lord Jesus Christ, you have made me and redeemed me and brought me to where I now am: you know what you wish to do with me; do with me according to your will, for your tender mercies' sake.'

✣ DAVID LIVINGSTONE
'O Lord, I am yours. Do what seems good
   in your sight,
and give me complete resignation to your
   will.'

✣ ANNE BRONTË
'In my Redeemer's name,
I give myself to thee;
And, all unworthy as I am,
My God will cherish me.'

✣ JANE AUSTEN
'Give us grace, almighty Father, to address you with all our hearts as well as with our lips.
   'You are present everywhere: from you no secrets can be hidden.
   'Teach us to fix our thoughts on you, reverently and with love, so that our prayers are not in vain, but are acceptable to you, now and always, through Jesus Christ our Lord.'

✣ JONATHAN SWIFT
'O almighty God, the searcher of all hearts, who has declared that who draw near to you with their lips when their hearts are far from you are an abomination to you: cleanse, we beseech you, the thoughts of our hearts by the inspiration of your Holy Spirit, that no wandering, vain, or idle thoughts may put out of our minds that reverence and godly fear that becomes all those who come into your presence.'

20 OF THE MOST FAMOUS PRAYERS

✚ THE GRACE

'The grace of the Lord Jesus Christ, the love of God, and the communion of the Holy Spirit be with all of you.'
2 CORINTHIANS 13:13 NRSV

✚ GETHSEMANE PRAYER

'Father, if you are willing, remove this cup from me; yet, not my will but yours be done.'
LUKE 22:42 NRSV

✚ PSALM 23

'The LORD is my shepherd, I shall not want.
    He makes me lie down in green pastures;
he leads me beside still waters;
    he restores my soul.
He leads me in right paths
    for his name's sake.

Even though I walk through the darkest valley,
    I fear no evil;
for you are with me;
    your rod and your staff –
    they comfort me.

You prepare a table before me
    in the presence of my enemies;
you anoint my head with oil;
    my cup overflows.
Surely goodness and mercy shall follow me
    all the days of my life,
and I shall dwell in the house of the LORD
    my whole life long.'
NRSV

✚ THE JESUS PRAYER

'Lord Jesus Christ, Son of God, have mercy on me, a sinner.'

✚ CHINESE STUDENT'S PRAYER

'O Lord, convert the world – and begin with me.'

✚ COLUMBA

'My dearest Lord,
be thou a bright flame before me,
be thou a guiding star above me,
be thou a smooth path beneath me,
be thou a kindly shepherd behind me,
today – tonight – and forever.'

✚ AUTHOR UNKNOWN

'O Lord, forgive what I have been, sanctify what I am, and order what I shall be.'

✚ THE LORD'S PRAYER

'Our Father, which art in heaven, hallowed be thy Name. Thy kingdom come. Thy will be done in earth, as it is in heaven. Give us this day our daily bread. And forgive us our trespasses, as we forgive them that trespass against us. And lead us not into temptation, but deliver us from evil. For thine is the kingdom, the power, and the glory, for ever and ever. Amen.'

✚ AUGUSTINE OF HIPPO

'Grant to us your servants: to our God – a heart of flame; to our fellow men – a heart of love; to ourselves – a heart of steel.'

'Almighty God, in whom we live and move and have our being, you have made us for yourself and our hearts are restless until in you they find their rest. Grant us purity of heart and strength of purpose, that no selfish passion may hinder us from knowing your will, no weakness from doing it; but that in your light we may see light clearly, and in your service we may find our perfect freedom; through Jesus Christ our Lord.'

✚ THE SERENITY PRAYER

'God, give us the serenity to accept what cannot be changed;
give us the courage to change what should be changed;
give us the wisdom to distinguish one from the other.'
ATTRIBUTED TO REINHOLD NIEBUHR

✠ BOOKMARK OF TERESA OF AVILA

'Let nothing disturb you
nothing frighten you,
all things are passing;
patient endurance
attains all things.
One whom God possesses
lacks nothing,
for God alone suffices.'

✠ SOLDIER'S PRAYER

'I asked God for strength, that I might
    achieve,
I was made weak, that I might learn
    humbly to obey.
I asked for health, that I might do greater
    things,
I was given infirmity, that I might do
    better things.
I asked for riches, that I might be happy,
I was given poverty, that I might be wise.
I asked for power, that I might have the
    praise of men,
I was given weakness, that I might feel
    the need of God.
I asked for all things, that I might enjoy
    life,
I was given life, that I might enjoy all
    things.
I got nothing that I asked for –
but everything that I had hoped for,
almost despite myself, my unspoken
    prayers were answered.
I am among all men most richly blessed.'

A SOLDIER'S PRAYER, WRITTEN BY AN ANONY-
MOUS CONFEDERATE SOLDIER, IN THE US CIVIL WAR

✠ LORD ASTLEY

'O Lord, thou knowest how busy I must be
this day. If I forget thee, do not thou forget
me.'

GENERAL LORD ASTLEY, BEFORE THE BATTLE OF
EDGEHILL

Richard of Chichester – statue erected at Chichester Abbey to commemorate the millennium.

✠ RICHARD OF CHICHESTER

'Thanks be to you, my Lord Jesus Christ,
for all the benefits you have won for me.
For all the pains and insults you have
    borne for me.
O most merciful Redeemer, Friend, and
    Brother,
may I know you more clearly,
love you more dearly,
and follow you more nearly,
day by day.'

✠ BENEDICT

'Father,
give us wisdom to perceive you,
intellect to understand you,
diligence to seek you,
patience to wait for you,
eyes to behold you,
a heart to meditate on you
and a life to proclaim you,
through the power of the Spirit
of our Lord Jesus Christ.'

✠ RAVENSBRÜCK PRAYER

'O Lord, remember not only the men and women of good will, but also those of ill will. But do not remember all the suffering they have inflicted on us; remember the fruits we have brought, thanks to this suffering – our comradeship, our loyalty, our courage, our generosity, the greatness of heart which has grown out of all this, and when they come to judgment let all the fruits which we have borne be their forgiveness.'

PRAYER FOUND NEAR THE BODY OF A DEAD CHILD IN THE RAVENSBRÜCK CONCENTRATION CAMP

✠ DESIDERIUS ERASMUS

'Lord Jesus Christ, you said that you are
the Way, the Truth, and the Life.
Help us not to stray from you, for you are
the Way;
nor to distrust you, for you are the Truth;
nor to rest on any other than you, as you
are the Life.
You have taught us what to believe, what
to do, what to hope, and where to
take our rest.
Give us grace to follow you, the Way, to
learn from you, the Truth, and live
in you, the Life.'

✠ BOOK OF HOURS

'God be in my head,
and in my understanding;
God be in my eyes,
and in my looking;
God be in my mouth,
and in my speaking;
God be in my heart,
and in my thinking;
God be at my end,
and at my departing.'

WRITTEN IN 1514

✠ JOHN CHRYSOSTOM

'Almighty God, who hast given us grace at this time with one accord to make our common supplications unto thee; and dost promise, that when two or three are gathered together in thy Name thou wilt grant their requests; fulfil now, O Lord, the desires and petitions of thy servants, as may be most expedient for them; granting us in this world knowledge of thy truth, and in the world to come life everlasting. Amen.'

TIMES FOR PRAYER

✠ EARLIEST REFERENCE TO PRAYING THREE TIMES A DAY

The *Didache*, a 2nd-century Christian manual about morals and church practice regarding baptism and the Lord's Supper, told Christians to pray three times a day.

✠ FIRST REFERENCE TO SERVICES HELD FOUR TIMES A DAY

The 4th-century pilgrim, Egeria, reported that she found on a trip to Jerusalem that monks attended services four times a day.

✠ LITERAL OBEDIENCE TO PSALM 119:164

Psalm 119:164 states, 'Seven times a day I praise you.' Monasteries in the 4th century based their seven daily services of prayer on this Bible verse. Their seven services were: Lauds, Prime, Terce, Sext, None, Vespers and Compline.

.4 SIGNS AND SYMBOLS

Early Christians were often severely persecuted because they refused to worship the Roman Emperors. They identified themselves by the use of secret signs and sought refuge in the underground burial places, the catacombs.

The term 'symbol' refers to a concrete sign or figure which recalls the idea of a spiritual reality. Jesus himself used symbols to express the reality of God's presence; water was a symbol of God's Spirit, the dead fig-tree a symbol of God's punishment; the wine at Cana pictured his new life. The Christian church has continued to express God's love in pictures, songs and figures.

✤ LATIN ENIGMA

This intriguing set of letters has been found throughout the old Roman Empire, from Dura-Europos on the Euphrates in the east, to Cirencester, England in the west. The two oldest examples were found scratched on the walls of Pompeii, which means that they date back to before AD 79 when the city was destroyed in a volcanic eruption. The words can be spelled forwards and backwards in any column or line.

R	O	T	A	S	the wheels
O	P	E	R	A	with care
T	E	N	E	T	holds
A	R	E	P	O	Arepo
S	A	T	O	R	the sower

It can be translated as, 'The sower Arepo holds with care the wheels.' However, no one has found any sensible meaning to such a literal translation. The letters can be rearranged in a cross (see below) and then they make the words *Pater noster* (Our Father), in Latin, with *A* and *O* left over. These are the first and last letters of the Greek alphabet – Alpha and Omega – a New Testament designation of Christ.

✠ EARLIEST CHRISTIAN INSCRIPTION IN CATACOMBS

In Rome, the early Christians sought refuge from persecution in underground burial places, the catacombs, where they were able to worship in peace. The earliest known Christian inscription found there is dated AD 72.

FISH SYMBOL

These Greek words below mean: 'Jesus Christ, Son of God, Savior.'

✠ FIRST CHRISTIAN SECRET SYMBOL

The Greek word for fish, *ichthus*, formed an acrostic:

I	esous
CH	ristos
TH	eou
U	ios
S	oter

The symbol was simple to draw and was often used among Christians as a type of password during times of persecution by the Roman government. If two strangers met one of them might casually draw the shape of an arc in the earth. If the other were a Christian, he or she would complete the symbol with a reverse arc, forming the outline of a fish (see illustration).

✠ FIRST LITERARY REFERENCE

The fish as an ancient Christian symbol is known from the 1st-century catacombs in Rome. The first literary reference to a fish as a Christian symbol is from Clement of Alexandria (born c. 150) in *Paedogogus*, III, xi.

Early Christian sarcophagus from Rome marked with a fish, the Good Shepherd and an anchor.

INITIALS

✠ MOST USED INITIALS TO MARK TIME

The traditional way of marking time with BC – *Before Christ*, and AD – *Anno Domini* (In the year of our Lord), is no longer politically correct. The acceptable terms now are BCE – *Before the Common Era* and CE, *Common Era*.

✠ MOST MISINTERPRETED INITIALS

IHS – does not mean 'in his service.' These three letters are the first three capital letters of Jesus' name in Greek. IHSOUS pronounced ee-ay-soos means 'God is salvation.'

✠ LAST INITIALS USED OF JESUS

The initials *INRI* on a crucifix are initials for the Latin title that Pontius Pilate had written over the head of Jesus Christ on the cross. They are taken from the words recorded in John 19:19, 'JESUS OF NAZARETH, THE KING OF THE JEWS.' These words were written in Hebrew, Greek and Latin. In Latin, the official language of the Roman Empire, the words were 'Iesus Nazarenvs Rex Ivdaeorvm.'

The early Church adopted the first letters of each word of this inscription *INRI* as a symbol. Throughout the centuries *INRI* has appeared in many paintings of the crucifixion.

✠ J. S. BACH'S USE OF INITIALS

On the surviving manuscripts of the greatest composer for the organ, J. S. Bach, the initials 'J. J.' appear at the start of his compositions and they close with the initials, 'S. D. G.' They are abbreviations for the Latin, *Jesu Juva* (Jesus help me!) and *Soli Deo Gloria* (To the glory of God alone!).

SALVATION ARMY

✠ FIRST APPEARANCE

The Salvation Army Crest is a worldwide symbol of Christian compassion and service. The international crest first appeared in print in 1879. The design is credited to Captain William H. Ebdon.

Meaning of crest

The emblems in the crest symbolize Salvation Army doctrines:

- The round figure – the sun – represents the light and fire of the Holy Spirit.
- The cross in the center, the cross of Jesus Christ.
- 'S' stands for salvation.
- The swords, the warfare of salvation.
- The shots, the truths of the gospel.
- The crown, the crown of glory which God will give to all his soldiers who are faithful to the end.

ACROSTICS

Among the most popular acrostics concerning the Christian faith are:

✠ FAITH

F	louting
A	ppearances
I	
T	rust
H	im

F	orsaking
A	ll
I	
T	ake
H	im

F	eeling
A	fraid
I	
T	rust
H	im

F	aith
A	sks
I	mpossible
T	hings
H	umbly

✣ GOSPEL

The Gospel is:

G	ood news of God's grace to Guilty men.
O	ffered to all and Obeyed by faith.
S	alvation by a Substitionary Sacrifice.
P	eace and Pardon Proclaimed through Propitiation.
E	ternal life given to Everyone that believeth, with
L	ight, Liberty and Love.

✣ GRACE

G	od's
R	iches
A	t
C	hrist's
E	xpense

✣ PRAYER

Prayer consists of:

P	etition: '[Daniel] still prays three times a day.' (Daniel 6:13)
R	everence: 'Let us … worship God acceptably with reverence and awe.' (Hebrews 12:28)
A	doration: 'My lips will glorify you.' (Psalm 63:3)
Y	earning: 'Blessed are those who hunger and thirst for righteousness.' (Matthew 5:6)
E	xpectation: 'Elijah … prayed earnestly that it would not rain.' (James 5:17)
R	equests: 'Present your requests to God.' (Philippians 4:6)

✣ SCRIPTURE

All Scripture is given to:

S	anctify: 'Sanctify them through thy truth.' (John 17:17 KJV)
C	orrect: 'Profitable for correction.' (2 Timothy 5:16 KJV)
R	ejoice: 'Rejoicing the heart.' (Psalm 19:8 KJV)
I	nstruct: 'Instruction in righteousness.' (2 Timothy 3:16 KJV)
P	urity: 'Purified your souls in obeying the truth.' (1 Peter 1:22 KJV)
T	each: 'Teach me thy statutes.' (Psalm 119:12 KJV)
U	nite: 'Unite my heart to fear thy name.' (Psalm 86:11 KJV)
R	eprove: 'By them is thy servant warned.' (Psalm 19:11 KJV)
E	at: 'Thy words were found and I did eat them.' (Jeremiah 15:16 KJV)

✣ STEWARDSHIP

The faithful Christian

S	ees
T	hat
E	very
W	eek
A	
R	egular
D	onation
S	upports
H	is
I	ndividual
P	arish

SYMBOLS FROM THE EARLY CHRISTIANS

The early Christians lived in a mainly pagan and hostile society. During Nero's persecution (AD 64) their religion was considered 'a strange and illegal superstition.' The Christians were mistrusted and kept aloof, suspected and accused of the worst crimes, even cannibalism, because they talked about 'eating the flesh of Christ.' They were persecuted, imprisoned, sentenced to exile or condemned to death. Unable to profess their faith openly, the Christians made use of symbols, which they depicted on the walls of the catacombs and, more often, carved on the marble slabs which sealed the tombs.

✠ THE GOOD SHEPHERD
The Good Shepherd with a lamb around his shoulders represents Christ and the soul which he has saved. This symbol is often found on frescoes and statues.

✠ THE 'ORANTE'
The 'orante' was a female praying figure with open arms, extended in prayer, symbolizing the soul which lives in divine peace.

✠ MONOGRAM OF CHRIST
The monogram of Christ is formed by interlacing two letters of the Greek alphabet: X (*chi*) and P (*rho*), which are the first two letters of the Greek word 'Christòs' or Christ. When this monogram was placed on a tombstone, it meant a Christian was buried there.

✠ DOVE
The dove holding an olive branch symbolizes the soul that has reached divine peace.

✠ ALPHA AND OMEGA
The Alpha and the Omega are the first and the last letters of the Greek alphabet. They signify that Christ is the beginning and the end of all things.

✠ THE ANCHOR
The anchor is the symbol of salvation and of the soul which has peacefully reached the port of eternity.

THE PHOENIX
The phoenix, the mythical Arabian bird, which, according to the beliefs of the ancients, after a thousand years arises from its ashes, is the symbol of the resurrection of the body.

Loaves and fish – 5th-6th-century Roman mosaic at Tabgha, near Lake Galilee.

7.1
BIBLE
MARTYRS

Part 7

CHRISTIANS UNDER FIRE

7.2
APOSTOLIC
MARTYRS

7.3
EARLY
MARTYRS

7.4
FAMOUS
MARTYRS

7.5
THE BOXER
UPRISING

7.6
20TH-CENTURY
PERSECUTION

7.7
RESPONSES TO
ADVERSITY

7.1 BIBLE MARTYRS

The Greek word for 'witness' is *martus*, from which our word 'martyr' is derived. This translation comes a few times in the *King James Version* of the Bible: 'And when the blood of thy martyr Stephen was shed, I also was standing by' (Acts 22:20); '... in those days wherein Antipas was my faithful martyr ...' (Revelation 2:13).

The word 'martyr' came to mean a Christian who was killed because of his faith in Christ. So a martyr came to be a witness who was 'faithful, even to the point of death' (Revelation 2:10).

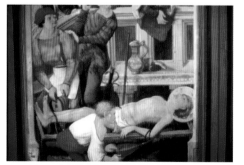

The martyrdom of St Vincent by fire and griddle.

✠ **MOST FAMOUS NON-MARTYRDOM**

The New Testament teaches that Christ's death on the cross was a sacrifice for sin, *not* a martyrdom.

OLD TESTAMENT MARTYRS

✠ **ZECHARIAH THE PRIEST**

'After the death of Jehoiada, the officials of Judah came and paid homage to the king, and he listened to them. They abandoned the temple of the LORD, the God of their fathers, and worshiped Asherah poles and idols. Because of their guilt, God's anger came upon Judah and Jerusalem. Although the LORD sent prophets to the people to bring them back to him, and though they testified against them, they would not listen.

'Then the Spirit of God came upon Zechariah son of Jehoiada the priest. He stood before the people and said, "This is what God says: 'Why do you disobey the LORD's commands? You will not prosper. Because you have forsaken the LORD, he has forsaken you.'"

'But they plotted against him, and by order of the king they stoned him to death in the courtyard of the Lord's temple. King Joash did not remember the kindness Zechariah's father Jehoiada had shown him but killed his son, who said as he lay dying, "May the LORD see this and call you to account."' 2 CHRONICLES 24:17-22

✠ **URIAH THE PROPHET**

'They brought Uriah out of Egypt and took him to King Jehoiakim, who had him struck down with a sword and his body thrown into the burial place of the common people.' JEREMIAH 26:23

Salome with the head of John the Baptist, by Bernardino Luini.

NEW TESTAMENT MARTYRS

✢ JOHN THE BAPTIST

(This is the only biblical account of the martyrdom of a relative of Jesus.)

'At that time Herod the tetrarch heard the reports about Jesus, and he said to his attendants, "This is John the Baptist; he has risen from the dead! That is why miraculous powers are at work in him."

'Now Herod had arrested John and bound him and put him in prison because of Herodias, his brother Philip's wife, for John had been saying to him: "It is not lawful for you to have her." Herod wanted to kill John, but he was afraid of the people, because they considered him a prophet.

'On Herod's birthday the daughter of Herodias [although her name is not mentioned in the Bible, Josephus, the Jewish historian, tells us her name: Salome] danced for them and pleased Herod so much that he promised with an oath to give her whatever she asked. Prompted by her mother, she said, "Give me here on a platter the head of John the Baptist." The king was distressed, but because of his oaths and his dinner guests, he ordered that her request be granted and had John beheaded in the prison. His head was brought in on a platter and given to the girl, who carried it to her mother. John's disciples came and took his body and buried it. Then they went and told Jesus.'

MATTHEW 14:1-12

✠ FIRST CHRISTIAN MARTYR

'Now Stephen, a man full of God's grace and power, did great wonders and miraculous signs among the people. Opposition arose, however, from members of the Synagogue of the Freedmen ... These men began to argue with Stephen, but they could not stand up against his wisdom or the Spirit by whom he spoke.

'Then they secretly persuaded some men to say, "We have heard Stephen speak words of blasphemy against Moses and against God."

'So they stirred up the people and the elders and the teachers of the law. They seized Stephen and brought him before the Sanhedrin. They produced false witnesses, who testified, "This fellow never stops speaking against this holy place and against the law. For we have heard him say that this Jesus of Nazareth will destroy this place and change the customs Moses handed down to us."

'All who were sitting in the Sanhedrin looked intently at Stephen, and they saw that his face was like the face of an angel.

'Then the high priest asked him, "Are these charges true?"

'To this Stephen replied: "Brothers and fathers, listen to me! The God of glory appeared to our father Abraham while he was still in Mesopotamia ... You stiff-necked people, with uncircumcised hearts and ears! You are just like your fathers: You always resist the Holy Spirit! Was there ever a prophet your fathers did not persecute? They even killed those who predicted the coming of the Righteous One. And now you have betrayed and murdered him – you who have received the law that was put into effect through angels but have not obeyed it."

'When they heard this, they were furious and gnashed their teeth at him. But Stephen, full of the Holy Spirit, looked up to heaven and saw the glory of God, and Jesus standing at the right hand of God. "Look," he said, "I see heaven open and the Son of Man standing at the right hand of God."

'At this they covered their ears and, yelling at the top of their voices, they all rushed at him, dragged him out of the city and began to stone him. Meanwhile, the witnesses laid their clothes at the feet of a young man named Saul.

'While they were stoning him, Stephen prayed, "Lord Jesus, receive my spirit." Then he fell on his knees and cried out, "Lord, do not hold this sin against them." When he had said this, he fell asleep.

'And Saul was there, giving approval to his death.'
Acts 6:8-15; 7:1-2, 51-60

✠ JAMES

(This is the only biblical record of the death of one of the first of the 12 apostles. Martyred around AD 30, the son of Zebedee was the brother of the apostle John.)

'It was about this time that King Herod [Herod Agrippa I] arrested some who belonged to the church, intending to persecute them. He had James, the brother of John, put to death with the sword.'
Acts 12:1-2

.2 APOSTOLIC MARTYRS

Jesus called 12 of his followers to be his apostles. Matthias was added to their number as a replacement for Judas Iscariot. When challenged, the apostle Paul claimed that his qualifications for being an apostle of Jesus were on the grounds that he had seen the risen Christ and that he had received a personal commission from him (see Acts 9:1-9; 1 Corinthians 15:8-10; Galatians 1:1,11-17.)

The Bible only gives details of the death of two of the apostles: Judas' suicide and James' execution by Herod. With the exception of John, according to tradition, all the other apostles were martyred.

THE 12 APOSTLES

✠ APOSTOLIC DEATHS
The only two apostolic deaths recorded in the Bible were Judas Iscariot, who betrayed Jesus and then went out and hanged himself and James the son of Zebedee, who was executed by Herod (Acts 12:2).

✠ PETER AND PAUL
Peter and Paul were most probably both martyred in Rome about AD 66, during the persecution under the Emperor Nero. Paul was beheaded. Peter was crucified, upside down at his request, since he did not feel he was worthy to die in the same manner as his Lord.

The martyrdom of St Andrew. Stained glass window in the church of St Ouen, Rouen, France.

✣ ANDREW

Tradition says that Andrew preached the gospel in what is now Russia and was crucified in Greece.

✣ THOMAS

Tradition says that Thomas went to India, where he was speared to death by four soldiers.

✣ PHILIP

Philip is supposed to have preached the gospel in Carthage in North Arica and then in Asia Minor, where he converted the wife of a Roman proconsul. For this the proconsul had Philip arrested and executed.

✣ MATTHEW

Tradition has Matthew preaching in Persia and Ethiopia. One tradition says that he was stabbed to death in Ethiopia.

✣ BARTHOLOMEW

By tradition Bartholomew traveled to India, Armenia, Ethiopia and Southern Arabia. He is said to have died a martyr's death.

✣ JAMES, THE SON OF ALPHEUS

James is supposed to have preached the gospel in Syria, where according to Jewish historian Josephus, he was stoned and then clubbed to death.

✣ SIMON THE ZEALOT

Tradition holds that Simon went to Persia and was martyred for refusing to sacrifice to the sun god.

✣ JUDAS, THE SON OF JAMES

This Judas, identified by John as 'Judas, not Iscariot,' was, according to one tradition, murdered by magicians in the city of Suanir in Persia. It is said that he was killed with clubs and stones.

✣ MATTHIAS

Matthias, who was chosen by the drawing of lots to replace Judas Iscariot, is said to have gone to Syria with Andrew where he was burned to death.

✣ THE ONLY APOSTLE NOT MARTYRED

(John was the only apostle 'deemed to be a martyr' but not martyred.)

'Being at Ephesus, he was ordered by the Emperor Domitian to be sent bound to Rome, where he was condemned to be cast into a cauldron of boiling oil. (This was a punishment which the philosopher Seneca refers to as being suitable for a slave who had been convicted of a very serious crime.) But here a miracle was wrought in his favor; the oil did him no injury, and Domitian, not being able to put him to death, banished him to Patmos, to labor in the mines, in AD 73. He was, however, recalled by Nerva, who succeeded Domitian, but was deemed a martyr on account of his having undergone an execution, though it did not take effect.'
JOHN FOXE, *THE BOOK OF MARTYRS*

.3 EARLY MARTYRS

William Bramley-Moore said that 'The history of Christian martyrdom is, in fact, the history of Christianity itself; for it is in the arena, at the stake, and in the dungeon that the religion of Christ has won its most glorious triumphs.' This section includes details about one of the slowest crucifixions, and martyrdom under Rome's cruellest emperor.

✣ ONE OF THE SLOWEST CRUCIFIXIONS

'This apostle and martyr (Andrew) was the brother of St Peter, and preached the gospel to many Asiatic nations. On arriving at Edessa, the governor of the country, named Egeas, threatened him for preaching against the idols they worshiped.

St Andrew, persisting in the propagation of his doctrines, was ordered to be crucified, two ends of the cross being fixed transversely in the ground. He boldly told his accusers that he would not have preached the glory of the cross had he feared to die on it. And again, when they came to crucify him, he said that he coveted the cross, and longed to embrace it. He was fastened to the cross, not with nails, but cords, that his death might be more slow. In this situation he continued two days, preaching the greatest part of the time to the people, and expired on the 30th of November.'

JOHN FOXE, *THE BOOK OF MARTYRS*

The Colosseum, Rome – the great arena used for public spectacles.

AN ANCIENT ENGLISH MARTYROLOGY

From an early period, the Christian church endeavored to keep alive and to celebrate the memory of its martyrs. They compiled martyrologies and remembered martyrs, usually on the anniversary of their death. This English Martyrology is compiled from manuscripts in the libraries of the British Museum and of Corpus Christi College, Cambridge. The figures in brackets are the age of the martyrs.

	MARTYR	PLACE OF MARTYRDOM	METHOD OF MARTYRDOM
JANUARY			
3	Anteros	Rome	Suffered martyrdom for Christ
20	Faianus	Rome	Suffered martyrdom for Christ
20	Marius	Rome	Suffered martyrdom for Christ
21	Agnes	Rome	Suffered martyrdom for Christ (13)
22	Anastasius	Persia	Beheaded
23	Emerentiana	Rome	Beheaded
24	Babyllas	Antochia	Beheaded
MARCH			
7	Perpetua & Felicitas	Carthage	Suffered martyrdom for Christ
23	Theodoretus	Antioch	Beheaded
APRIL			
9	Seven Women	Sirmium	Suffered martyrdom for Christ
14	Valerianus & Tiburtius	Rome	Beheaded
18	Eleutherius & Anthia	Rome	Killed with a sword
25	Mark	Alexandria	Dragged by a rope around his neck
28	Vitalis	Vicolongo	Burned alive
28	Christophorus	Samos	Beheaded
MAY			
3	Alexander	Rome	Stabbed to death
8	Victor	Milan	Beheaded
12	Pancratius	Rome	Beheaded (15)
14	Victor & Corona	Rome	Beheaded
20	Basilla	Rome	Killed with the sword
JUNE			
2	Marcellinus & Petrus	Rome	Beheaded
2	Arthemius	Rome	Killed with the sword
16	Ferreolus & Ferrucius	Besançon	Killed with the sword
17	Nicander & Blastus	Rome	Burned to death
18	Marcus & Marcellinus	Rome	Beheaded
19	Gervasius & Protasius	Milan	Beaten to death; beheaded
22	James the Less	Jerusalem	Killed by a weaver's beam
22	Alban	St Albans	Beheaded

	MARTYR	PLACE OF MARTYRDOM	METHOD OF MARTYRDOM
JULY			
7	Procopius	Caesarea	Beheaded
7	Marina	Antioch	Beheaded
10	Seven brothers	Rome	Killed by different tortures
10	Rufina & Secunda	Rome	Drowned in River Tiber
14	Phocas	Pontus	Thrown into a burning oven
17	Speratus	Carthage	Beheaded
19	Christina	Tyrus	Drowned at sea
AUGUST			
2	Theodota	Nicea	Burned to death
9	Romanus	Rome	Suffered martyrdom for Christ
10	Lawrence	Rome	Roasted alive
12	Euplius	Catania	Beheaded
13	Hipploytus	Rome	Dragged behind wild horses
17	Mommos	Caesarea	Stoned to death
22	Symphorianus	Autun	Beheaded
25	Bartholomew	India	Flayed alive
29	John the Baptist		Beheaded
30	Felix	Venusia	Beheaded
SEPTEMBER			
11	Protus & Hyacinthus	Rome	Beheaded
21	Matthew the apostle		Stabbed with a sword from behind
24	Andochius & Thyrsus	Gaul	Necks broken with cudgels
OCTOBER			
8	Dionysius	Paris	Beheaded
24	Sixteen soldiers	Fidenae	Beheaded
31	Quintinus	Rome	Beheaded
NOVEMBER			
8	Quattuor Coronati	Rome	Drowned in a locked lead chest
28	Saturninus	Toulouse	Dragged by a wild bull
30	Andrew	Patras	Crucified
DECEMBER			
13	Lucia	Rome	Beheaded
21	Thomas	India	Stabbed with sword, pierced with spears
25	Anastasia	Rome	A glorious martyrdom
26	Eugenia	Rome	Died in prison
26	Stephen	Jerusalem	Stoned to death

✤ MARTYRDOM UNDER ROME'S CRUELLEST EMPEROR

'When Herod Agrippa caused St James the Great to be put to death, and found that it pleased the Jews, he resolved, in order to ingratiate himself with the people, that Peter should be the next sacrifice. He was accordingly apprehended and thrown into prison; but an angel of the Lord released him, which so enraged Herod, that he ordered the sentinels who guarded the dungeon in which he had been confined to be put to death. St Peter, after various miracles, retired to Rome, where he defeated the artifices and confounded the magic of Simon Magus, a great favorite of the Emperor Nero: he likewise converted to Christianity one of the minions of that monarch, which so exasperated the tyrant, that he ordered both St Peter and St Paul to be apprehended. During the time of their confinement, they converted two of the captains of the guard and 47 other people to Christianity. Having been nine months in prison, Peter was brought from thence for execution, when, after being severely scourged, he was crucified with his head downwards; which position, however, was at his own request.'

JOHN FOXE, *THE BOOK OF MARTYRS*

✤ PAUL

'At Iconium, St Paul and St Barnabas were near being stoned to death by the enraged Jews; on which they fled to Lycaonia. At Lystra, St Paul was stoned, dragged out of the city, and left for dead. He, however, happily revived, and escaped to Derbe. At Philippi, Paul and Silas were imprisoned and whipped; and both were again persecuted at Thessalonica. Being afterwards taken at Jerusalem, he was sent to Caesarea, but appealed to Caesar at Rome. Here he continued a prisoner at large for two years; and at length, being released, he visited the churches of Greece and Rome, and preached in France and Spain. Returning to Rome, he was again apprehended, and, by the order of Nero, martyred, by beheading.

'About this same time saints James, Philip, Matthew, Mark, Matthias, Jude, Bartholomew, Thomas, and Luke the evangelist also suffered martyrdom for the cause of Christ.'

JOHN FOXE, *THE BOOK OF MARTYRS*

✤ JAMES THE RIGHTEOUS

This is the only account outside the Bible of the martyrdom of a relative of Jesus. This James, not to be confused with one of the 12 apostles, who was referred to as James the brother of John, was known as 'the Lord's Brother', 'the Just' and 'the Righteous'. The risen Jesus appeared to him (see 1 Corinthians 15:7) and this presumably helped him to believe in Jesus, for in John's Gospel it is recorded that `For even his own brothers did not believe in him [Jesus]' (John 7:5).

'After Paul had successfully appealed to Caesar and was sent off to Rome the disappointed Jews turned their attention to James. They hatched this plot against the Lord's brother, whom the apostles had appointed to the episcopal throne at Jerusalem. They hauled James up in front of a great crowd and demanded that he deny Christ. To their surprise James remained calm and showed unexpected tranquillity before this hostile crowd. James openly declared that our Savior and Lord, Jesus, was indeed the Son of God. They were unable to stomach this testimony as James was universally acclaimed as a most righteous man.

'Clement tells us that they seized James, threw him off a parapet and then clubbed him to death.'

EUSEBIUS, *THE HISTORY OF THE CHURCH*

4 Famous Martyrs

The martyrdom of John Hus, the 'morning star of the Reformation,' is recorded in John Foxe's *The Book of Martyrs*. Part of it says, 'After the ceremony of degradation the bishops delivered him to the emperor, who handed him over to the Duke of Bavaria. His books were burnt at the gates of the church; and on July 6th he was led to the suburbs of Constance to be burnt alive.' This section also records the first English martyr, the archbishop martyred in his own cathedral, the martyrdom of the greatest compiler of Christian liturgy, and the martyrdom of one of the most famous Bible translators.

✠ CZECHOSLOVAKIA'S MOST FAMOUS MARTYR

'When [John] Hus was brought before the council he was accused of 26 heresies. The council pronounced him a heretic condemning him to be burned as such, unless he recanted. Hus was then thrown into a filthy prison, where, during the day, he was so laden with chains that he could hardly move, and at night was fastened by his hands to a ring on the prison wall.

'Soon after Hus had been condemned four bishops and two lords were sent by the emperor to the prison, in order to prevail on Hus to recant. But Hus called God to witness, with tears in his eyes, that he was not conscious of having preached or written anything against God's truth, or against the faith of his orthodox church. The deputies then represented the great wisdom and authority of the council: to which Hus replied, "Let them send the meanest person of that council, who can convince me by argument from the word of God, and I will submit my judgment to him." The deputies, finding they could not make any impression on him, departed, greatly astonished at the strength of his resolve.

'After the ceremony of degradation the bishops delivered him to the emperor, who handed him over to the Duke of Bavaria. His books were burnt at the gates of the church; and on July 6th he was led to the suburbs of Constance to be burnt alive. Having reached the place of execution, he fell on his knees, sung several portions from the Psalms, and looked steadfastly towards heaven, saying, "Into thy hands, O Lord! do I commit my spirit: thou hast redeemed me, O most good and faithful God."

'As soon as the chain was put around him at the stake, he said, with a smiling countenance, "My Lord Jesus Christ was bound with a harder chain than this for my sake: why, then, should I be ashamed of

John Hus.

this old rusty one?" Then he prayed: "Lord Jesus Christ, it is for the sake of the gospel and the preaching of the word that I patiently undergo this ignominious death."

'When the faggots were piled around him, the Duke of Bavaria was officious as to desire him to abjure. "No," he said, "I never preached any doctrine of an evil tendency; and what I taught with my lips I now seal with my blood." He then said to the executioner, "You are now going to burn a goose (the meaning of Hus's name in Bohemian), but in a century you will have a swan whom you can neither roast nor boil." If this were spoken in prophecy, he must have alluded to Martin Luther, who came about a hundred years after him, and had a swan for his arms.

'As soon as the faggots were lighted, the martyr sang a hymn, with so cheerful a voice, that he was heard above the cracklings of the fire and the noise of the multitude. At length his voice was interrupted by the flames, which soon put an end to his existence. His ashes were collected, and, by order of the council, thrown into the Rhine, lest his adherents should honor them as relics.'

JOHN FOXE, THE BOOK OF MARTYRS

✠ MARTYR WHO IMPRESSED JOHN BUNYAN

In his copy of Foxe's *Book of Martyrs* that he had with him during his 12-year imprisonment, Bunyan wrote under the story of John Hus:

'Heare is John Hus that you may see,
Uesed in deed with all crulity;
But now leet us follow and look one him,
whear he is full field in deed to the brim.'

ENGLISH MARTYRS

✠ FIRST ENGLISH MARTYR

The city of St Albans derives its name from the first English martyr, the proto-martyr. In 304 a Roman soldier, Alban, was stationed at Verulamium, a Roman town.

During the persecutions of Emperor Severus, a priest called Amphibalus was on the run. He arrived in Verulamium looking for shelter. Alban took Amphibalus into his house even though Alban was not a Christian himself. Alban took note of the hours the priest spent in prayer. He then asked Amphibalus to instruct him in his faith and became a Christian. Alban was soon denounced as a protector of Christians. Soldiers were sent to search his house, but Alban heard they were on the way. So he gave Amphibalus his clothes and let him out of his house through a secret door. Alban had just time to put on the priest's clothes before the soldiers arrived. He was taken before a judge where his disguise was quickly unmasked. When Alban was asked to offer sacrifice to Jupiter and Apollo, he replied, 'I confess Jesus Christ, the son of God, with my whole being. Those whom you call gods are idols; they are made with hands.' Alban was beheaded on a hill overlooking the city of Verulamium.

✠ ARCHBISHOP MARTYRED IN HIS OWN CATHEDRAL

1170 saw the fateful killing of Archbishop Thomas Becket by Henry II's knights, on the steps leading up to the Canterbury Cathedral's high altar. Less than three years later Becket was declared a saint and pilgrims flocked to his grave in their thousands.

Today the spot of Becket's murder is marked by a six inch square stone. On a wall nearby the following words are carved:

Thomas Becket
Archbishop. Saint. Martyr.
Died here
Tuesday 29th December
1170

✠ GREATEST COMPILER OF LITURGY

Thomas Cranmer was Archbishop of Canterbury and the main compiler of the *Book of Common Prayer*. In Queen Mary's reign he was tried and condemned to be executed for being a heretic. Before his execution, he signed recantations of the beliefs which were really his. He was martyred on the 21st March 1556.

'When the wood was kindled, and the fire began to burn near him, stretching out his arm, he put his right hand into the flame, which he held so steadfast and immovable that all men might see his hand burned before his body was touched. His body did so abide the burning of the flame, with such constancy and steadfastness, that standing always in one place, without moving his body, he seemed to move no more than the stake to which he was bound: he eyes were lifted up unto heaven, and often times he repented his unworthy right hand, so long as his voice would suffer him: and using often the words of Stephen, "Lord Jesus receive my spirit"; in the greatness of the flame he gave up the ghost.'
JOHN FOXE, *THE BOOK OF MARTYRS*

✠ MARTYRED FOR TRANSLATING THE BIBLE

'William Tyndale was condemned by a decree issued from Augsburg by the emperor. Tyndale was taken to be executed and as he was being tied to the stake, he cried with a loud and earnest voice, "Lord, open the King of England's eyes!" He was then strangled, and his remains burnt to ashes. Such was the power and excellence of this truly good man, that during his imprisonment he converted the jailor, and his daughter, and others in his employment. Several of them who came into contact with him during his imprisonment said of him, that if he were not a good Christian, they did not know whom to trust; and the procurator-general left this testimony about him, that he was "a learned, a good, and a godly man."'
JOHN FOXE, *THE BOOK OF MARTYRS*

The murder of Archbishop Thomas Becket, Canterbury Cathedral.

THE BOXER UPRISING IN CHINA

It is estimated that over 32,000 Chinese Christians (30,000 Catholics and 2,000 Protestants) were killed by the Boxers, a fiercely nationalistic Chinese secret society, as they stormed through China, chanting their imperial command, 'Exterminate the Christian religion! Death to the foreign devils!' Never had so many Protestant missionaries been killed in the field in one year. In 1900, 135 missionaries and 53 missionary children were killed in China, of whom 79 were linked to the China Inland Mission (CIM).

Leaders in Yuh-Shan church who kept the church going during the enforced absence of missionaries through the Boxer trouble.

THE BOXERS

Thirteen missionaries from the American Board, which sponsored and supported Congregationalists from America to be missionaries in China, were killed in the Boxer uprising of 1900 in North China. The following letter from Mrs Atwater, published in *The Times* on October 15, 1900, bears partial testimony to the thousands of Chinese Christians who were massacred in 1900.

'... For Boxers were sweeping through the city, massacring the native Christians and burning them alive in their homes ... As the patrol was passing a Taoist temple on the way, a noted Boxer meeting-place, cries were heard within. The temple was forcibly entered. Native Christians were found there, their hands tied behind their backs, awaiting execution and torture; some had already been put to death, and their bodies were still warm and bleeding. All were shockingly mutilated. Their fiendish murderers were at their incantations burning incense before their gods, offering Christians in sacrifice to their angered deities.'

✤ BLIND CHANG

Chang Men was one example of the many thousands of Chinese Christians who died during the Boxer uprising of 1900. Chang became blind in his thirties and his character was then accurately summed up by his nickname 'Wu so pu wei te,' meaning, 'one without a particle of good in him'. His neighbors believed that he had been struck blind as a judgment on his evil way of life. He threw his wife and daughter out of his home, gambled, stole and became a womanizer.

When Chang learnt that blind people were being cured at a mission hospital he went there. As a result he received both physical and spiritual sight. He longed to be

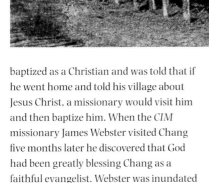

Martyr's graves, 1990.

baptized as a Christian and was told that if he went home and told his village about Jesus Christ, a missionary would visit him and then baptize him. When the *CIM* missionary James Webster visited Chang five months later he discovered that God had been greatly blessing Chang as a faithful evangelist. Webster was inundated with over 400 people wanting to become Christians.

Later Chang lost his eyesight again, after a Chinese doctor operated on him, in an attempt to improve his partial sight. However, this did not deter Chang, who became well-known as the itinerant blind Christian evangelist, able to quote nearly all of the New Testament by heart, as well as many complete chapters from the Old Testament. The Boxer rebels came across blind Chang in Tsengkow, in Manchuria. The Boxers captured 50 Christians there but were told that for every one they killed a further 10 would appear, and that they needed to deal with the ringleaders of the Christians, blind Chang. The Boxers said that they would free their 59 Christian prisoners if one of them would tell them where blind Chang was. No one betrayed blind Chang, but one of the 50 managed to escape and went and told Chang what was happening.

Blind Chang went to the Boxers at once. He refused to worship the god of war in the temple. Chang was herded into an open cart and paraded through the town to a cemetery outside the city. As he went through the crowds, Chang sang a song he had learned in the Christian hospital:

Jesus loves me, He who died
Heaven's gate to open wide;
He will wash away my sin,
Let His little child come in.

Jesus loves me, He will stay,
Close beside me all the way;
If I love Him when I die,
He will take me home on high.

The last words blind Chang uttered, as the Boxer's sword gleamed in the sun on its way to decapitating him, were, 'Heavenly Father, receive my spirit.'

CIM Magazine, 1901

Chinese mandarins in council, 1875-6, before the Boxer uprising.

20TH-CENTURY PERSECUTION

The Christian martyrs of the 20th century are the forgotten martyrs. Most Christians who live in countries where Christians are not martyred know little about the extent of persecution their fellow-Christians have to endure. It has been estimated that there have been more Christians martyred in the 20th century than in all the previous centuries put together.

CHINA

In 1999 China intensified its attack on religion as the government further clamped down on unofficial gatherings of house-churches, prayer and Bible study.

On August 18, and August 23, 1999, officers from China's Public Security Bureau (PSB) raided various homes in Henan province, and arrested 39 Christian leaders.

The first raid took place in the city of Wu Gang where eight men were holding an 'illegal' Bible class. All their money and their Bibles were confiscated. Christian meetings outside the registered churches are considered to be 'illegal religious activities.'

The second police raid occurred on the afternoon of August 23, 1999 in Tanghe county, in southwestern Henan Province, when 31 house church leaders were arrested as they gathered for a Bible study in a farmer's home. It is believed that an informant reported the meeting place to the authorities.

Two of the 31 detained Christians were sent back to their home county of Fangcheng, where they remain in jail. The other 29 were detained at the Public Security Detention Center in Nanyang.

MARTYRS IN INDIA

Mr Graham Stewart Staines and his wife faithfully served as missionaries with the Evangelical Missionary Society of Mayurbhanj for more than 30 years, working mostly among lepers.

Mr. Staines, a 58-year-old Australian missionary, and his two sons, Philip (age ten) and Timothy (age eight) were asleep inside their vehicle when it was doused with gasoline and set ablaze. All three were killed. From the reports it is clear that the three were murdered because it was well known that they were Christians. The attack took place in Manoharpur village in the District of Keonjhar in the State of Orissa. The militants believed to be responsible are the radical Hindu nationalist group *Rashtriya Swayamsevak Sangh (RSS)*.

✣ PERSECUTION IN INDIA

In 1999 persecution in India was horrific. Pastors and Catholic priests were:
- stripped and paraded naked,
- Bibles burned,
- churches razed to the ground or ransacked and set ablaze,
- Catholic nuns gang-raped
- Christian institutions attacked.

In 1999 more than 100 churches were destroyed.

WESTMINSTER ABBEY, LONDON

On July 10, 1998, stone sculptures of 10 modern Christian martyrs were dedicated on the medieval front of Westminster Abbey. Models for the statues were carefully designed by Tim Crawley from records and photographs of the martyrs. Under his general direction the figures have been carved from French Richemont limestone by him and by Neil Simmons, John Roberts and Andrew Tanser. The statues were unveiled on July 9, 1998 by the Archbishop of Canterbury in the presence of H.M. The Queen, H.R.H. The Duke of Edinburgh and church leaders and representatives from many parts of the world.

These 20th-century martyrs are from every continent and many Christian denominations.
- **Grand Duchess Elizabeth of Russia**, of the Orthodox Church, who was killed by the Bolsheviks in 1918.
- **Oscar Romero**, the Roman Catholic archbishop of El Salvador, who was assassinated in 1980.
- **Maximilian Kolbe** of Poland, a Franciscan friar who was killed by the Nazis in 1941.

Westminster Abbey, London, and statues on the west façade of modern-day martyrs Archbishop Romero and Dietrich Bonhoeffer.

This list of countries indicate where there is known persecution or severe discrimination against Christians.

Algeria	Israel	Philippines
Azerbaijan	Jordan	Romania
Bangladesh	Kazakhstan	Russia
Bhutan	Kuwait	Rwanda
Burma	Laos	Saudi Arabia
China	Latvia	Sri Lanka
Colombia	Libya	Sudan
Cuba	Macedonia	Turkey
Egypt	Mexico	Vietnam
Ethiopia	Morocco	Uzbekistan
Germany	Nepal	Yemen
Haiti	Nigeria	
India	North Korea	
Indonesia	Pakistan	
Iran	Peru	

- The Anglican, **Manche Masemola**, a 16-year-old convert in South Africa who was killed by her animist parents in 1928.
- **Lucian Tapiedi**, killed in 1942 during the Japanese invasion of Papua New Guinea.
- **Janani Luwum**, a Ugandan archbishop assassinated during the rule of Idi Amin in 1977.
- **Dietrich Bonhoeffer**, a German Lutheran pastor and theologian, killed in 1945 by the Nazis.
- **Wang Zhiming**, a Chinese pastor and evangelist, who was killed in 1972 during the Cultural Revolution.
- **Esther John**, a Presbyterian evangelist in Pakistan, killed in 1960.
- Probably the most famous martyr is **Dr Martin Luther King**, who took religion as the ideological platform to bring about change in America in the 1960s. One of the world's most famous civil rights activists, he was a Baptist minister. He was assassinated in 1968, age 39.

155

7.7 RESPONSES TO ADVERSITY

Quotations about suffering and dying for Christ, as well as quotations of those who have died for what they believe, have been collected together here. Jesus left his followers in no doubt that they would be liable to persecution if they followed him. The apostle Paul echoed this teaching when he wrote to his young protégé, Timothy: 'In fact, everyone who wants to live a godly life in Christ Jesus will be persecuted' (2 Timothy 3:12).

PERSECUTION

✠ FIRST PROMISE THAT CHRISTIANS WILL BE PERSECUTED

'They persecuted me, they will persecute you.'

JESUS CHRIST, JOHN 15:20

✠ WORLDWIDE PERSECUTION

'Everyone who wants to live a godly life in Christ Jesus will be persecuted.'

THE APOSTLE PAUL, 2 TIMOTHY 3:12

✠ IGNATIUS

'I am the wheat of God, and am ground by the teeth of the wild beasts, that I may be found the pure bread of God.'

IGNATIUS, BISHOP OF ANTIOCH, IN ABOUT AD 100, URGED BELIEVERS IN THEIR LOVE FOR HIM NOT TO ATTEMPT TO HAVE HIM RELEASED FROM PRISON. HE MET HIS DEATH [FROM WILD BEASTS] AT ROME UNDER THE REIGN OF EMPEROR TRAJAN (AD 98-117)

✠ LUTHER

'If the Devil were wise enough and would stand by in silence and let the gospel be preached, he would suffer less harm. For when there is no battle for the gospel it rusts and it finds no cause and no occasion to show its vigor and power. Therefore, nothing better can befall the gospel than that the world should fight it with force and cunning.'

QUOTES FROM MARTYRS

✣ **ALBAN**

When asked to offer sacrifice to Jupiter and Apollo, Alban replied, 'I confess Jesus Christ, the son of God, with my whole being. Those whom you call gods are idols; they are made with hands.'

✣ **RAMON LULL**

'I desire to be a fool that I may give honor and glory to God, and I will have no art nor device in my words by reason of the greatness of my love.'

RAMON LULL, WHO DELIGHTED TO CALL HIMSELF THE FOOL OF LOVE, WAS AN INFLUENTIAL WRITER AND MISSIONARY IN THE MIDDLE AGES. HE WAS MARTYRED IN 1315 OR 1316

✣ **JOAN OF ARC**

'If I were to say that God had not sent me, I would be damning myself, for it is true that God did send me.'

✣ **JEROME OF PRAGUE**

When his executioner went behind him to set fire to the stakes, he said, 'Come here and kindle it before my eyes; for had I been afraid of it, I would not have come here, having had so many opportunities to escape.'

When the flames enveloped him he sang a hymn, ending with the words: '*Hanc animam in flammis affero, Christe, tibi!*' ('This soul in flames I offer, Christ, to thee!')

✣ **JOHN HUS**

Hus said to his executioner: 'You are now going to burn a goose (the meaning of Hus's name in Bohemian), but in a century you will have a swan whom you can neither roast nor boil.'

✣ **LATIMER**

'Be of good comfort, Mr Ridley, and play the man! We shall this day light such a candle, by God's grace, in England, as I trust never shall be put out.'

LATIMER'S WORDS TO RIDLEY AS A STAKE WAS SET ON FIRE AT HIS FEET

William Tyndale.

✣ **WILLIAM TYNDALE**

'Lord, open the King of England's eyes!'

✣ **THOMAS CRANMER**

'I recant of my recantations.'

✣ **SIR THOMAS MORE**

'I die the King's good servant, but God's first.'

MORE, FROM THE SCAFFOLD

✣ **CHARLES I**

'I go from a corruptible to an incorruptible crown, where no disturbance can be.'

✣ **JIM ELLIOT**

'He is no fool who gives up what he cannot keep to gain what he cannot lose.'

JIM ELLIOT WROTE THE ABOVE AS A STUDENT. HE WAS SPEARED TO DEATH AT THE HANDS OF THE AUCA INDIANS, JANUARY 8, 1956

✣ **NAMELESS MARTYRS**

Justin Martyr became convinced about the truth of Christianity through the faithful witness of Christian martyrs. Justin wrote: 'For I myself, too, when I was delighting in the doctrines of Plato, and heard the Christians slandered, and saw them fearless of death ... perceived that it was impossible that they could be living in wickedness and pleasure.'

Part 8

POTPOURRI

8.1
CHRISTMAS

8.2
EASTER

8.3
CHURCH
BUILDINGS

8.4
MYSTERY OF
THE SHROUD

8.5
IN MEMORIAM

8.1 CHRISTMAS

The festival of Christ's birth has been celebrated in the Western Church on December 25 since about the 4th century. The Eastern Orthodox Church celebrates Christmas on January 6, and links it with the season of Epiphany, when Christ was manifested to the world by the Magi (wise men).

In many western countries, Christmas has been so commercialized and secularized that it is often hard to find any reference to the nativity story. Christians have not always celebrated Christmas. Some Puritans refused to have a holiday on Christmas Day.

Washington Christmas tree.

✥ UNKNOWN DATE OF THE BIRTH OF JESUS

The exact date of Jesus' birth is not known, but according to the Gospels he was born near the end of Herod the Great's reign. Since Herod died in 4 BC, Jesus was probably born shortly before, around 5 or 6 or 7 BC.

✥ ORIGIN OF CHRISTMAS TREES

The evergreen, traditionally spruce, decorated Christmas tree originated in Germany, where it was known from the 16th century.

✥ THE WASHINGTON CHRISTMAS TREE

There has been a large Christmas tree on the White House lawn in Washington since the 1920s. Each year the President turns on its lights.

✥ THE TRAFALGAR SQUARE TREE

Every year since the end of World War II a tall fir tree from Oslo has been shipped to London and set up in Trafalgar Square, London. The people of Norway do this in gratitude for the help Britain gave them in the last world war.

✥ TALLEST CHRISTMAS TREE

The world's tallest cut Christmas tree was a 221 foot high Douglas fir (*Pseudotsuga menziessii*) which was erected in December 1950 at Northgate Shopping Center, Seattle, Washington.

CAROL SINGING

Many churches in England have a Christmas service with the Christmas story told with readings from the Bible, interspersed with the singing of carols.

They often model their services on the annual Festival of Nine lessons and Carols which is televised live on Christmas Eve from King's College Chapel, Cambridge. The service always starts with a boy chorister singing a solo from the carol *Once in royal David's city*.

Towns in the US have different traditions about singing carols. In Boston carol singers are accompanied by hand-bell players on Beacon Hill. In New Orleans hundreds of people gather in Jackson Square on December 22 for community carol singing.

CHRISTMAS CARDS

✣ FIRST CHRISTMAS CARD

The earliest known printed Christmas card was made for an Englishman, Sir Henry Cole, in 1843.

✣ MOST PROLIFIC SENDER OF CHRISTMAS CARDS

Werner Erhard of San Francisco, California, sent out 62,824 personal Christmas cards in December 1975.

✣ CHRONOLOGY OF THE CELEBRATION OF CHRISTMAS

Date	Event
4th century	Emperor Constantine builds Church of Nativity in Bethlehem and declares Christ's birthday an official Roman holiday. The Bishop of Rome establishes December 25 as the day to celebrate Christ's birth. Nicholas, bishop of Myra, lives in Turkey. In the Middle Ages his feast day is December 6, and he is known as a giver of gifts and the patron saint of children.
6th century	The church sets apart the four Sundays preceding Christmas for devotional preparation – Advent begins.
8th century	Boniface, English missionary to the Germans, replaces sacrifices to Oden's oak with a fir tree adorned in tribute to the Christ child.
11th century	Word 'Christmas' first used in English.
13th century	Francis of Assisi ministers to illiterate, poor people by introducing a live nativity scene into the church and festive carols in the language of the people.
17th century	First mention of Christmas tree in Germany. In 1644 English law under the Puritans makes December 25 an official work day, and observance of Christmas was made illegal.
18th century	Handel's *Messiah* written in 24 days.
Mid-19th century	Modern Christmas begins to take shape. Clement Moore's *A Visit from St Nicholas* (later known as *The Night Before Christmas*) popularizes Santa Claus. Prince Albert introduces the Christmas tree to England. Christmas cards become a tradition.

Carol singing around the Christmas tree, Trafalgar Square, London.

8.2 EASTER

Easter is the annual Christian festival celebrating the resurrection of Jesus. The earliest mention of Easter occurs in correspondence between the bishops of Rome and Smyrna, dating to AD 154. It is clear from these letters that a holy day to celebrate Jesus' resurrection was widely observed at that time. Unlike Christmas Day, the date for Easter Day changes each year. It is now celebrated on the first Sunday after the full moon, following the spring equinox. It falls between March 22 and April 23.

✠ IN THE BIBLE

The word 'Easter' is never mentioned in the original Scriptures. However, the *King James Version* translates Acts 12:4 as follows: 'And when he [Herod the King] had apprehended him [Peter], he put him in prison, and delivered him to four quaternions of soldiers to keep him; intending after Easter to bring him forth to the people.'

The Greek word which the *King James Version* translates as 'Easter' is actually the word *Pascha* which means 'Passover.' The *New King James Version* says, 'So when he had arrested him, he put him in prison, and delivered him to four squads of soldiers to keep him, intending to bring him before the people after Passover.'

✠ DATE OF EASTER

The Council of Nicea in 325, fixed the date of Easter so that it would supersede an old pagan festival. It stated that it should be celebrated on the Sunday following the first full moon after the spring equinox.

✠ OBERAMMERGAU'S PASSION PLAY

The Passion Play, based on the life of Christ, dates from the 17th century. It was first performed in 1634, following a vow taken by the people of Oberammergau during an outbreak of bubonic plague, which killed 15,000 nearby Munich residents in 1634 - 1635.

The frightened population of Oberammergau prayed to be spared, taking a vow to be fulfilled not by a few but by the whole community. They vowed to do something in which everyone, rich and poor alike, would have a part: a Passion Play, the most sacred of all stories. They would present the story of Christ to the world every 10 years for evermore if the Lord would remove the plague from their people.

Oberammergau passion play: part of the cast's costume department.

The town was spared, and a tradition was born.

The play is now performed at the start of each decade. Although the cast is huge – 1,700 parts – performers must be Oberammergau natives, or have lived there for 10 years, or been married to a native and lived there for at least ten years.

The crowd shout against Jesus.

8.3 CHURCH BUILDINGS

Between 1200 and 1400 nearly 200 Gothic style cathedrals were built in western Europe. They reflect many aspects of the Christian faith in medieval times. The flying buttresses, soaring spires, and pointed arches show a reaching up to heaven. The magnificent stained glass windows depict scenes and people from the Christian gospel. These towering structures, often built on the highest part of the city, emphasize the mystery and magnificence of God.

The Liberty Bell.

BELLS

✢ FIRST WIDESPREAD USE OF CHURCH BELLS

At the beginning of the 7th century, church bells began to be used to call people to worship and to give the hours to the monks in the monasteries.

✢ OLDEST BELL TOWER

The bell tower of St Benedict Church, Rome, is inscribed with the date, 'anno domini millesimo sexagesimo IX' (1069).

✢ HEAVIEST SWINGING BELL

Cologne Cathedral has a bell which weighs 25.4 tons. It is the world's heaviest swinging bell.

✢ HEAVIEST AMERICAN BELL

Bourdon, Riverside Church, New York, has a bell cast in 1931 weighing 18.54 tons.

✢ THE BELL INSCRIBED WITH LEVITICUS 25:10

The bell that proclaimed freedom, the Liberty bell, is in Philadelphia and has part of Leviticus 25:10 inscribed on it: 'Proclaim liberty throughout all the land unto all the inhabitants thereof.' The bell was cast in England in 1752 by order of the Pennsylvania Assembly in honor of the 50th anniversary of the founding of Pennsylvania. It was rung on July 8, 1776, to celebrate the first public reading of the Declaration of Independence on July 4, 1776. The bell weighs about 2,080 pounds and is 12 feet in circumference round the lip. According to tradition, it first cracked in 1835 while tolling for the funeral of Chief Justice Marshall. It cracked beyond repair in 1846 when it was rung for George Washington's birthday. That was the last time it was heard.

STAINED GLASS

✤ CHARTRES CATHEDRAL

With the Gothic development in the 1140s the art of stained glass begins to replace mural painting as the basic decoration. This entire window at the west end of Chartres Cathedral, located above the famous Royal Portals, is devoted to the Tree of Jesse. It is one of the earliest major works of stained glass.

✤ OLDEST STAINED GLASS

The world's oldest complete stained glass is in the Cathedral of Augsburg, Germany. It dates back to the 11th century and depicts the biblical prophets.

✤ LARGEST STAINED GLASS WINDOW

The Resurrection Mausoleum in Justice, Illinois, houses the world's largest stained glass window. It consists of 2,448 panels and covers an area of 22,381 square feet.

✤ LARGEST AREA OF STAINED GLASS

The largest area of stained glass, consisting of more than a single window, is in York Minster, York, England. The stained glass covers 25,000 square feet.

Chartres Cathedral, France, and the South Rose window.

CATHEDRAL AND CHURCHES

✤ OLDEST RIB VAULTING

Durham Cathedral, England, begun in 1093 and completed toward 1130, has the oldest example of rib vaulting in any church.

✤ OLDEST ORTHODOX PARISH IN AMERICA

Holy Trinity Cathedral, San Francisco, is the oldest Orthodox parish in the contiguous United States.

✤ OLDEST CHURCH IN 'LONDON'

St Paul's Anglican Cathedral is the oldest church in London, Ontario, Canada.

Greenstead Church, England – the oldest parish church in the world.

✤ OLDEST CHRISTIAN CHURCH

The oldest undisputed Christian church dates back to AD 231, at Dura-Europos on the Euphrates where one room of a private house was altered to make room for up to 100 people. Its wall paintings included Adam and Eve, the Good Shepherd, Jesus walking on water and David and Goliath.

✤ OLDEST UK CATHEDRALS

CATHEDRAL	FOUNDED
Canterbury	1071
Lincoln	1073
Rochester	1077

✤ OLDEST AMERICAN CHURCHES

CHURCH	BUILT
Cervento de Porta Coeli, San German, Puerto Rico	1609
San Estevan del Rey Mission, Valencia County, New Mexico	1629
St Luke's Church, Isle of Wight County, Virginia	1632

✤ CATHEDRAL WITH MOON ROCK

The only cathedral to have on display a piece of moon rock is the Washington National Cathedral. It is the sixth largest cathedral in the world, and has a stained glass window commemorating the Apollo 11 moon landing.

✤ OLDEST PIECE OF WORKING MACHINERY

Salisbury Cathedral is home to an ancient clock mechanism dating from 1386. It does not have a clock face, but strikes on the hour. It is the oldest working clock and claims to be the oldest piece of machinery in the world.

Facing page: Western façade of Cologne Cathedral, Germany.

Durham Cathedral, England.

Facing page: The imposing interior of Cologne Cathedral, Germany.

✣ ISLAND CATHEDRALS

There are four Scottish cathedrals currently in use for worship which stand on offshore islands. The four cathedrals are on: the islands of Cumbrae, Lismore, Iona and Orkney.

✣ CATHEDRAL WITH ITS PRIVATE TIME ZONE

Christ Church, Oxford, keeps time by the Oxford meridian, while the main college clock in Tom Tower keeps the statutory (Greenwich) time, 5 minutes in advance. So all services start five minutes late because they go by Christ Church time.

✣ HIGHEST CATHEDRALS OF THE 13TH CENTURY

- Notre Dame de Paris was 114 feet high.
- Chartres Cathedral was 123 feet high.
- Amiens Cathedral was 138 feet high.
- Beauvais Cathedral was 157 feet high, before it collapsed.

✣ LONGEST CRYPT

The Civil War Memorial Church in the Guadarrama Mountains, Spain, has an underground crypt 853 feet in length.

✣ GARGOYLES

A gargoyle is a grotesquely carved human or animal figure found on an architectural structure.

They were made to look ugly in the belief that frightening figures scared away evil spirits. Gargoyles were originally designed to be spouts to throw rainwater clear of buildings.

THE LARGEST...

✣ CATHEDRAL

The largest cathedral in the world is St John the Divine Cathedral, New York. It has a floor area of 121,000 square feet and the world's longest nave, 414 feet long.

✣ CHURCH

The world's largest church is the Basilica of St Peter, Rome. It is 717 feet long and has a floor area of 247,572 square feet.

✣ BRITISH CHURCH

Westminster Abbey, the Collegiate Church of St Peter in Westminster, to give it its official title, is 503 feet long and 203 feet wide.

✣ GERMAN CATHEDRAL

Cologne Cathedral is the largest cathedral in Germany. Its west tower reaches 512 feet and the whole building is 144 feet long.

✣ LONGEST BRITISH NAVE

St Albans Cathedral, with its nave of 285 feet, has the longest nave of any English cathedral.

✣ SECOND LARGEST CATHEDRAL

The Liverpool Anglican Cathedral, the second largest cathedral in the world, was designed by Giles Gilbert Scott, who was also responsible for the classic English red telephone box.

Exterior and interior of Ulm Cathedral. The spire dominates the city.

✣ SMALLEST CATHEDRAL

The smallest cathedral in the world, measuring only 14 feet by 17 feet, and seating only 18 people, is Christ Catholic Church, Highlandville, Missouri.

SPIRES

✣ TALLEST CATHEDRAL SPIRE

The tallest cathedral spire is on the Protestant Cathedral of Ulm, Germany. It is 528 feet high.

✣ TALLEST ENGLISH CATHEDRAL SPIRE

Salisbury Cathedral hosts the tallest spire in England. 404 feet high, the cathedral's spire was added 100 years after its consecration and its immense weight, some 6,000 tons, meant that the cathedral needed much strengthening.

Salisbury Cathedral was built within one lifetime (1220-1258), a rarity for medieval cathedrals.

✣ TALLEST CHURCH SPIRE

Chicago Temple of the First Methodist Church, Clark Street, Chicago, Illinois, has the world's highest spire. It is on top of a 22-storey skyscraper. The tip of its steeple is 568 feet above street level.

4 MYSTERY OF THE SHROUD

One of the most absorbing mysteries of modern times revolves around the Turin Shroud. No other cloth in history from anywhere in the world has been so studied, examined and debated as the mysterious Shroud of Turin. Many believe that it is the cloth which was wrapped over Jesus' head as he lay in the tomb. When the Shroud of Turin went on display in 1988 for the first time in 20 years, it made the cover of *Time* magazine under the heading: 'Is this Jesus?' This entry examines the evidence of carbon dating and comes to a conclusion about the authenticity of the Turin Shroud. The supposed mystery of the Turin Shroud has now been solved: at least to the satisfaction of some scientists who have made a painstaking study of it.

TURIN SHROUD

✠ CARBON-DATING

Although radiocarbon tests have dated the shroud to AD 1260-1390, no one had been able to account for the shadowy image of a naked, 6-foot-tall man that appears on the shroud.

With bloodstains on the back, wrists, feet, side and head, the image appears to be that of a crucified man. Details such as the direction of the flow of blood from the wounds, the placement of the nails through the wrists rather than the palms, reveal a knowledge of crucifixion that seems too accurate to have been that of a medieval artist.

✠ COSMIC ENERGY?

A number of art historians have made careful assessments about the nature of the

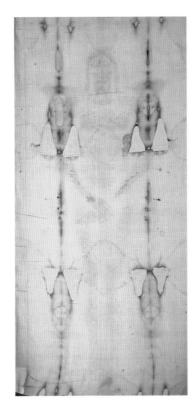

Flat view of the shroud.

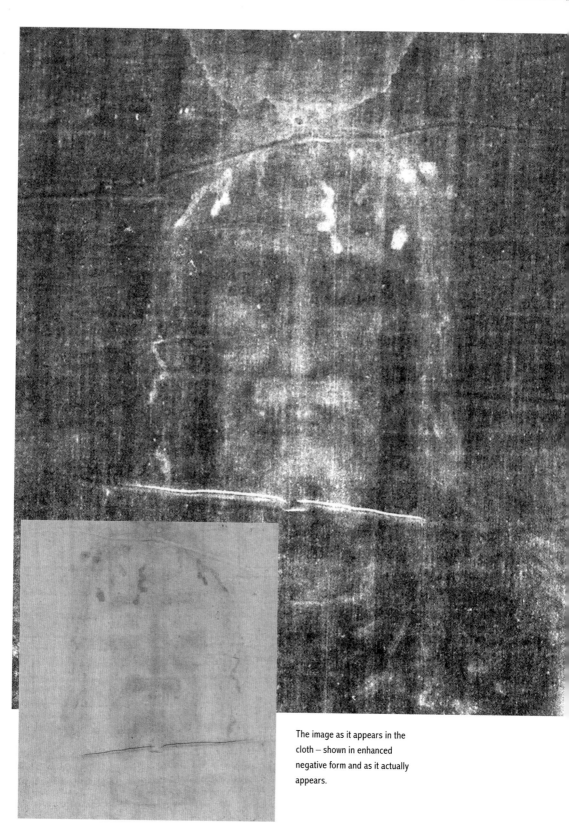

The image as it appears in the
cloth – shown in enhanced
negative form and as it actually
appears.

Turin Shoud. They agree on one thing: 'The Turin Shroud does not look like any other known work of art.' The implication drawn from this is that its creation was somehow miraculous. It has been postulated that the image may have been made by a sudden burst of cosmic energy as the cloth came into contact with the dead body of Jesus.

✤ *ACHEIROPOIETAI*

The Shroud of Turin belongs to the long tradition of sacred objects that are both relic and icon.

These kinds of objects first appeared in the 6th century, in the Holy Land. In Greek they are called *acheiropoietai*, that is, 'not made by human hands.'

They are given this name because they are, apparently, contact impressions of holy bodies and are not the work of any artists. They became relics through physical contact with the sacred and became icons because of the images they possessed.

✤ VERONICA'S VEIL

The most characteristic form of *acheiropoietos* is the holy cloth. Veronica is supposed to have stepped forward to wipe the sweat from Jesus' brow as he fell carrying his cross. The tradition is that her towel miraculously retained the image of Jesus' face. This became known as *Veronica's Veil*, and was revered as one of the most famous *acheiropoietai* of the Middle Ages.

✤ TURIN SHROUD'S IMAGE

The image on the Shroud of Turin *appears* to be produced by blood, blood plasma and sweat absorbed from Jesus' dead body at the time of entombment. According to *Time Magazine* in 1997 'no one has been able to account for the image' on the Turin Shroud.

✤ THE EXPLANATION

In 1979 Walter C. McCrone (President of the McCrone Research Institute which specializes in teaching and researching into applied microscopy, refractometry and microchemistry) took 32 samples from the shroud. Each sample contained more than 1,000 linen fibers and any materials attached to the shroud. Standard forensic tests to check for blood were made on these samples. No trace of blood was found. The paint pigment, red ochre, made up the body and blood images. The blood images came from another pigment, vermilion. Both red ochre and vermilion were in common use in the Middle Ages.

✤ REVELATIONS OF X-RAY DIFFRACTION

In 1980 the Electron Optics Group at McCrone Associates used electron and x-ray diffraction and found red ochre (iron oxide, hematite) and vermilion (mercurie sulfide); their electron microprobe analyzer found iron, mercury, and sulfur on a dozen of the blood-image area samples. These results fully confirmed Dr McCrone's results and further proved that the image had been painted twice – once with red ochre, followed by vermilion to enhance the blood-image results.

✤ GRISAILLE PAINTING

Grisaille, a style of faint, monochrome painting, similar to the painting on the Turin Shroud, was common in the 14th century.

8.5 IN MEMORIAM

Mourning in biblical times was openly expressed by shrieking, weeping and wailing. 'Joseph threw himself upon his father and wept over him and kissed him' (Genesis 50:1). Mourners tore their clothes, fasted and rubbed dirt into their faces and hair. Sometimes professional mourners were hired to express a family's grief. 'When they came to the home of the synagogue ruler, Jesus saw a commotion, with people crying and wailing loudly' (Mark 5:38).

The Christian hope of life with Jesus after death puts a new perspective on the after-life.

Charles Dickens.

FAMOUS BURIAL PLACES

✛ **WASHINGTON NATIONAL CATHEDRAL**
▪ Helen Keller 1880-1968
▪ Anne Sullivan 1866-1936
Helen Keller became known as an American memoirist and lecturer. Blind and deaf since infancy, she learned to read, write, and speak from her teacher Anne Sullivan who, visually impaired herself, lectured widely on behalf of sightless people.

✛ **WESTMINSTER ABBEY**
Charles Dickens' grave, in Poet's Corner, attracts particular interest. As a writer he drew attention to the hardships borne by the socially deprived and advocated the abolition of the slave trade. A wreath is still laid on his tomb each year on the anniversary of his death.

John and Charles Wesley
In Westminster Abbey there is a monument to John and Charles Wesley. On part of the tablet there is a representation of John Wesley preaching from his father's tomb in Epworth churchyard. Underneath are his words, 'I look upon all the world as my parish.' There is, in addition, a well-known saying of Charles Wesley: 'God buries his workmen, but carries on His work.'

EPITAPHS

✛ **EMILY DICKINSON**
'Called Back'
WEST CEMETERY; AMHERST, MASSACHUSETTS, SELF WRITTEN

✛ **C. S. LEWIS**
'Man must endure his going hence.'
HEADINGTON QUARRY CHURCHYARD; OXFORDSHIRE, ENGLAND

✠ JOHN BERRIDGE

'Here lie the earthly remains of John
Berridge, the late vicar of Everton, and an
itinerant servant of Jesus Christ, who loved
his Master and his work, and after running
on his errands many years was called to
wait on him above.
Reader, art thou born again?
No salvation without new birth!
I was born in sin, February 1716.
Remained ignorant of my fallen state
till 1730.
Lived proudly on faith and works
for salvation till 1754.
Was admitted to Everton Vicarage, 1755.
Fled to Jesus alone for refuge, 1756.
SELF WRITTEN

✠ MARTIN LUTHER KING

'Free at last, free at last
Thank God A'mighty I'm free at last.'

✠ JOHN NEWTON

'John Newton, Clerk,
Once an infidel and libertine,
A servant of slaves in Africa:
Was by the rich mercy of our Lord
and Saviour, Jesus Christ,
Preserved, restored, pardoned,
And appointed to preach the Faith
He had long laboured to destroy.
Near sixteen years at Olney in Bucks:
And twenty-seven years in this Church.'

THE CRYPT OF THE POPES

The following inscriptions are from the
Crypt of the Popes, Rome. It was discovered
by the great archeologist de Rossi in 1854,
and called by him 'the little Vatican, the
central monument of all Christian ceme-
teries.' It originated toward the 2nd
century as a private crypt. Its sepulchers,
now empty, once contained the remains of
nine popes and eight 3rd-century bishops.

On two tombstones are the abbreviation
MRT ('martyr,' which means 'witness').
This title was given to the Christians who
had witnessed to their faith in Christ by
shedding their blood.

✠ TWO POEMS BY ST DAMASUS (366-384)

On the right-hand wall of the Crypt of the
Popes there are two original fragments of a
poem by Damasus, celebrating Sixtus II's
martyrdom:

'At the time when the sword
(persecution)
pierced the bowels of the Mother
(Church),
I,(now) buried here, taught as pastor
the Word of God (the divine Scriptures).
When suddenly the soldiers rushed in,
dragged me from the (episcopal) chair.
The faithful offered their necks to the
sword,
But as soon as the Pastor saw the ones
who wished to rob him of the palm (of
martyrdom)
he was the first to offer himself
and his own head, not tolerating
that the (pagan) frenzy should harm the
others.
Christ, who gives recompense,
made manifest the Pastor's merit,
preserving unharmed the flock.'

'BIBLE' EPITAPHS

Over the centuries Christians have used
phrases from the Bible to express their
certain hope in the resurrection life. (The
quotations are often a slight paraphrase of
the precise Bible verse.)

- 'The Lord is my Shepherd.' PSALM 23:1.
- 'I know that my Redeemer liveth.'
  JOB 19:25.
- 'Because I live, ye shall live also.'
  JOHN 14:19.
- 'Mine eyes have seen thy salvation.'
  LUKE 2:30.
- 'We which have believed do enter into
  rest.' HEBREWS 4:3.
- 'I give unto them eternal life; and they
  shall never perish.' JOHN 10:28.
- 'The gift of God is eternal life through
  our Lord Jesus Christ.' ROMANS 6:23.

Part 9

CENTURY-BY-CENTURY CHRONOLOGY

9.1
1ST TO 5TH
CENTURIES

9.2
6TH TO 14TH
CENTURIES

9.3
15TH TO 17TH
CENTURIES

9.4
18TH TO 20TH
CENTURIES

9.1 1ST TO 5TH CENTURIES

All the writings of the New Testament were probably completed by the end of the 1st century. Before Constantine became emperor Christians were frequently tortured and martyred because they refused to offer incense to the Roman gods. Tacitus records their great courage: 'First those who confessed to being Christians were arrested, then, on information obtained from them, hundreds were convicted, more for their anti-social beliefs than for fire-raising. In their deaths they were made a mockery. They were covered in skins of wild animals, torn to death by dogs, crucified or set on fire – so that when darkness fell they burned like torches in the night.'

1st CENTURY

The Acts of the Apostles records the dynamic expansion of Christianity in the 1st century. From being a tiny group of frightened followers of Jesus, hiding behind locked doors in Jerusalem, they became fearless preachers who 'caused trouble all over the world' (Acts 17:6). For two years, the gospel of Jesus was preached 'boldly and without hindrance' by the fearless apostle Paul in the center of the known world, Rome, for two years (Acts 28:30-31). In less than 30 years Paul helped to establish Christianity along the main roads and in the chief cities of the Empire, from Antioch to Rome. The prophecy recorded in the first chapter of Acts 1:8, 'You will be my witnesses in Jerusalem, and in all Judea and Samaria, and to the ends of the earth' had been literally fulfilled by the end of the 1st century.

2nd CENTURY

✠ **MOST FAMOUS EARLY MARTYR**
'Eighty and six years have I served Him, and he never did me any injury; how then can I blaspheme my King and my Savior.'
POLYCARP

✠ SIGNIFICANT EVENTS IN THE 1st CENTURY

- Life, death, and resurrection of Jesus.
- Jerusalem destroyed by the Romans.
- The words and sayings of Jesus collected and preserved.
- New Testament writings completed.
- Times of persecution. Nero blames Christians for a devastating fire that ravages the city in AD 64.

✠ ONE OF THE EARLIEST
DESCRIPTIONS OF CHRISTIANS

'They dwell in their own countries but
simply as sojourners. As citizens, they
share in all things with others, and yet
endure all things as if foreigners. Every
foreign land is to them as their native
country, and every land of their birth as a
land of strangers. They marry, as do others;
they beget children; but they do not destroy
their offspring. They have a common table
but not a common bed. They are in the
flesh, but they do not live after the flesh.
They pass their days on earth, but are citizens
of heaven. They obey the prescribed
laws, and at the same time surpass the laws
in their lives. They love all, and are persecuted
by all. They are poor, yet they make
many rich; they are completely destitute,
and yet they enjoy complete abundance.

✠ SIGNIFICANT EVENTS
IN THE 2nd CENTURY

- Martyrdom of Polycarp in 155.
- Justin Martyr beheaded in 165.
- Montanism rises in Phrygia in 175 – a charismatic
  movement which emphasized new
  revelations.
- According to Eusebius Christianity came to
  Britain by the end of the 2nd century.

The martyrdom
of Polycarp.

Mosaic roundel
with Christian
Chi-Rho from a
Roman villa,
Dorset, England,
4th century.

- In the 4th century the Christian church had taken root in countries stretching from Spain in the West to Persia and India in the East.
- Constantine becomes Emperor, (306-337), professes Christianity and the church was given legal status.
- The first major council of church held in Nicea in 325.
- Augustine converted in 386. He became one of the most important theologians in all of church history.
- Patrick (c. 390-460) goes to evangelize Ireland.
- Monasticism arose in Egypt in the 3rd and 4th centuries and was organized in the East by St Basil the Great (c. 330-379) and, later, in the West by St Benedict (480-547).

They are reviled, and yet they bless. When they do good they are punished as evil-doers; undergoing punishment, they rejoice because they are brought to life.'
EPISTLE TO DIOGNETUS, AUTHOR UNKNOWN, WRITTEN ABOUT AD 130

✠ FIRST GREAT CHRISTIAN PHILOSOPHER

'You can kill us, but you can't hurt us.'
JUSTIN MARTYR (c.100-c.165)

3rd TO 5th CENTURIES

✠ PRAYER OF GREATEST OF THE CHURCH FATHERS

'Almighty God, in whom we live and move and have our being, you have made us for yourself and our hearts are restless until in you they find their rest. Grant us purity of heart and strength of purpose, that no selfish passion may hinder us from knowing your will, no weakness from doing it; but that in your light we may see light clearly, and in your service we may find our perfect freedom; through Jesus Christ our Lord.'
AUGUSTINE (354-430)

✠ PATRICK'S MOST FAMOUS PRAYER

'I rise today with the power of God to
    guide me,
the might of God to uphold me,
the wisdom of God to teach me,
the eye of God to watch over me,
the ear of God to hear me,
the word of God to give me speech,
the hand of God to protect me,
the path of God to lie before me,
the shield of God to shelter me,
the host of God to defend me
against the snares of the devil and the
    temptations of the world,
against every man who meditates injury
    to me,
whether far or near.'
THE BREASTPLATE OF ST PATRICK

6TH TO 14TH CENTURIES

The middle age of Christianity has often been called 'the Dark Ages,' though it was neither a 'dark' age, nor an 'age of faith.' Popes Gregory VII and Innocent III built the papacy into perhaps the greatest institutional achievement of the Middle Ages. The medieval spirituality of Aquinas, which he developed into a full-blown systematic theology, was enhanced by the piety of Bernard of Clairvaux and Francis of Assisi.

Bede.

6th TO 9th CENTURIES

✠ MOST INFLUENTIAL 'RULE'

'Idleness is the enemy of the soul. Therefore, at fixed times, the brothers should be busy with manual work; and at other times engage in holy reading. This ought to be ordered in the following way: from Easter until 1 October, on leaving *Prime*, they shall work until the fourth hour. From the fourth hour until the sixth hour they devote themselves to reading. After the meal at the sixth hour they shall rest in silence on their beds.'
EXTRACT FROM BENEDICT'S *RULE*

✠ FIRST CHRISTIAN KING IN WESSEX, ENGLAND

'No wise man wants a soft life.'
KING ALFRED THE GREAT (849-899)

'Lord God Almighty, shaper and ruler of all creatures, we pray that by your great mercy and by the token of the holy cross you will guide us to your will. Make our minds steadfast, strengthen us against temptation, and keep us from all unrighteousness. Shield us against our enemies, seen and unseen. Teach us to inwardly love you before all things with a clean mind and a clean body. For you are our Maker and Redeemer, our help and comfort, our trust and hope, forever.'
KING ALFRED THE GREAT (849-899)

✠ MOST TALENTED HISTORIAN OF THE EARLY MIDDLE AGES

'He alone loves the Creator perfectly who manifests a pure love for his neighbor.'
VENERABLE BEDE (c. 673-735)

'I beseech Thee, good Jesus, that as Thou hast graciously granted to me here on earth sweetly to partake of the words of Thy wisdom and knowledge, so Thou wilt vouchsafe that I may some time come to Thee, the fountain of all wisdom, and

always appear before Thy face; who livest
and reignest, world without end.'
Venerable Bede (c. 673-735)

✤ GREATEST THEOLOGIAN OF THE 8th CENTURY

'The day of resurrection!
Earth, tell it out abroad;
The passover of gladness,
The passover of God!
From death to life eternal,
From earth unto the sky,
Our Christ hath brought us over
With hymns of victory.'
John of Damascus (c. 675-c. 749)

10th TO 14th CENTURIES

✤ 14th-CENTURY SPIRITUALITY

'Lord, make me an instrument of your
peace.
Where there is hatred, let me sow love,
where there is injury, pardon,
where there is doubt, faith,
where there is despair, hope,
where there is darkness, light,
where there is sadness, joy.

O Divine Master, grant that we may not
so much seek
to be consoled as to console,

not so much to be understood as to
understand,
not so much to be loved as to love.
For it is in giving that we receive,
it is in pardoning that we are pardoned,
it is in dying that we are born to eternal
life.'
Attributed to Francis of Assisi
(c. 1181-1226)

✤ SIGNIFICANT EVENTS IN THE 6th TO 9th CENTURIES

- Columba (c. 521-597) goes as missionary to Scotland. Mission headquarters at Iona.
- 529 Benedict of Nursa establishes monastery of Monte Cassino and the Benedictine Order.
- Mohammed (c. 570-c. 632) begins the religion of Islam: begins to supplant Christianity across the Middle East and North Africa.
- c. 575-79 Gregory sees English youths in Rome and asks if he may be allowed to evangelize the English.
- 596 Gregory, now pope, sends Augustine on a mission to the English.
- 601 Pope Gregory makes Augustine Archbishop of Canterbury, and sends helpers for a mission, including Paulinus, who preached to King Edwin in Northumbria.
- Alfred the Great (849-899), is King of Wessex in England. Translated Christian writings into the language of the common people. Devoted half his time and money to religious purposes.

Francis of
Assisi.

✠ MOST NOTABLE MEDIEVAL MONK

In answer to an inquiry from an official in Rome, Bernard of Clairvaux described in detail four degrees of the Christian's love. They are:

1. Man loves himself for his own sake.
2. Man loves God but for his own advantage.
3. Man loves God for God's sake.
4. Man loves himself for the sake of God.

✠ LEADING SCHOLAR OF THE 14th CENTURY

The chronicler Fuller records Wycliffe's influence:

'They burnt his bones to ashes
and cast them into the Swift,
a neighboring brook running hard by.
Thus the brook hath conveyed his ashes
  into Avon,
Avon into Severn; Severn into the
  narrow seas;
and they into the main ocean.
And thus the ashes of Wycliffe are the
  emblem
of his doctrine which now is dispersed
  the world over.'

✠ SIGNIFICANT EVENTS IN THE 10th TO 14th CENTURIES

- Benedictine monastery established 909 at Cluny; becomes the center of a reform movement for the church.
- 1009 Moslems sack Holy Sepulcher in Jerusalem.
- As a result of differences and rivalry between East and West, the unity of the church is broken. After the great schism of 1054 the church is split into the Orthodox Church in the East, and the Catholic Church in the West.
- Bernard of Clairvaux (1090-1153) and his reforming and devotional writing.
- 1095 Pope Urban II proclaims the First Crusade to reclaim Jerusalem from the Moslems.
- 1115 Bernard establishes monastery at Clairvaux. He will become the 'greatest churchman of the 12th century.'
- 1147 Second Crusade (supported by Bernard of Clairvaux) fails, with many Crusaders dying in Asia Minor.
- 1154 Election of Adrian IV, the only English pope
- 1170 Pope Alexander III established rules for the canonization of saints. Thomas à Becket is murdered in England.
- 1187 Loss of Jerusalem by the Crusaders.
- 1194 Chartres Cathedral begun.
- 1209 Francis of Assisi establishes Franciscans.
- 1272 Thomas Aquinas summarizes Scholastic Theology in his *Summa Theologica,* writing, 'I believe, that I may understand.'
- 1382 John Wycliffe is expelled from Oxford University, translates Bible into English, and trains lay preachers to spread the Scripture.
- 1398 John Hus begins lecturing on theology at Prague University and spreads Wycliffe's ideas.

9.3 15TH TO 17TH CENTURIES

Like many aspects of the Crusades of previous centuries, the dark days of the Spanish Inquisition remain a stain on the record of Christianity. The Reformers are sometimes categorized by the vehemence of their protests against the Roman Catholic Church. In many ways the Anglicans and Martin Luther were the most conservative in their treatment of medieval piety and theology, while John Calvin, from his base in Geneva, was less conservative, and the Anabaptists, who rejected infant baptism and practiced the baptism of adults upon confession of faith in Jesus, were the most radical.

15th CENTURY

✣ LEADING DEVOTIONAL WRITER
'Jesus has many who love his kingdom in heaven, but few who bear his cross. He has many who desire comfort, but few who desire suffering. He finds many to share his feast, but few his fasting. All desire to rejoice with him, but few are willing to suffer for his sake. Many follow Jesus to the breaking of bread, but few to the drinking

✠ SIGNIFICANT EVENTS IN THE 15th CENTURY

- 1414-1417 The Council of Constance seeks to end the Great Schism, the embarrassment of having two or three popes competing for authority and power. Council burns Czech priest John Hus as a heretic and condemns John Wycliffe posthumously.
- c. 1415-1424 Thomas à Kempis' classic *The Imitation of Christ* written.
- 1431 France – Joan of Arc burned at Rouen as a witch.
- 1453 The Turks capture Constantinople and turn St Sophia Basilica into a mosque.

- c. 1453 Johannes Gutenberg develops his printing press and prints the first Bible.
- 1479 The Inquisition against heresy in Spain set up by Ferdinand and Isabella with papal approval.
- Florence under the Medicis becomes the center of Renaissance humanism.
- Michelangelo, Botticelli, and Leonardo da Vinci create important works of art with Christian themes.
- 1492 Columbus' voyage and a new age of exploration and Christian expansion begins.

The vast ceiling of the Sistine Chapel, completed in four years by Michelangelo.

of the cup of his passion. Many admire his miracles, but few follow him to the humiliation of his cross.

'They who love Jesus for his own sake, and not for the sake of comfort for themselves, bless him in every trial and anguish of heart, no less than in the greatest joy. And were he never willing to bestow comfort on them, they would still always praise him and give him thanks.'

THOMAS À KEMPIS, *THE IMITATION OF CHRIST*,

16TH CENTURY

✠ MOST INFLUENTIAL PERSON AFTER COLUMBUS

Ralph Waldo Emerson, 300 years after Luther (1483-1546), asserted: 'Martin Luther the Reformer is one of the most extraordinary persons in history and has left a deeper impression of his presence in the modern world than any other except Columbus.'

✠ MOST IMPORTANT BOOK OF THE CENTURY

The first edition of John Calvin's summary of the Protestant faith, *Institutes of the Christian Religion*, was published at Basle in 1536.

'Original sin may be defined as the hereditary corruption and depravity of our nature. This reaches every part of the soul, make us abhorrent to God's wrath and

Oliver Cromwell.

✠ SIGNIFICANT EVENTS IN THE 16th CENTURY

- In 1517 Martin Luther nails his 95 theses to the church door in Wittenberg.
- Luther's translation of the Bible into German and Tyndale's into English.
- The Protestant Reformation spreads throughout Europe with Zwingli and John Calvin in Switzerland, the Anabaptists in central Europe, and John Knox in Scotland.
- The Counter-Reformation defends traditional Catholicism against Reformation ideas. The Council of Trent (1545-1563) re-affirms Catholic doctrine. The Jesuit order sends missionaries abroad.
- Foxe's *Book of Martyrs* records the persecution of believers.
- In England, the Puritans become influential.

produces in us what Scripture calls works of the flesh.'

JOHN CALVIN, *INSTITUTES OF THE CHRISTIAN RELIGION*, 1:1:8

✠ MOST IMPORTANT FIGURE OF THE COUNTER-REFORMATION

Ignatius Loyola (1491-1556), a converted soldier, became a wandering pilgrim and spiritual guru, often imprisoned by the church authorities on suspicion of heresy.

'Dearest Lord, teach me to be generous; teach me to serve you as you deserve; to give and not to count the cost, to fight and not to heed the wounds, to toil and not to seek for rest, to labour and not to seek reward, except to know that I do your will.'

IGNATIUS LOYOLA

186

17TH CENTURY

✠ MOST FAMOUS CHRISTIAN ALLEGORICAL BOOK

'Now I saw in my dream, that the highway up which Christian was to go, was fenced on either side with a wall, and that wall was called Salvation, Isaiah 26:1. Up this way, therefore, did burdened Christian run, but not without great difficulty, because of the load on his back.

'He ran thus till he came at a place somewhat ascending; and upon that place stood a cross, and a little below, in the bottom, a sepulcher. So I saw in my dream, that just as Christian came up with the cross, his burden loosed from off his shoulders, and fell from off his back, and began to tumble, and so continued to do till it came to the mouth of the sepulcher, where it fell in, and I saw it no more.

'Then was Christian glad and lightsome, and said with a merry heart, "He hath given me rest by his sorrow, and life by his death." Then he stood still a while, to look and wonder; for it was very surprising to him that the sight of the cross should thus

John Bunyan.

ease him of his burden. He looked, therefore, and looked again, even till the springs that were in his head sent the waters down his cheeks, Zech. 12:10. Now as he stood looking and weeping, behold, three Shining Ones came to him, and saluted him with, "Peace be to thee." So the first said to him, "Thy sins be forgiven thee," Mark 2:5; the second stripped him of his rags, and clothed him with change of raiment, Zech. 3:4; the third also set a mark on his forehead, Eph. 1:13, and gave him a roll with a seal upon it, which he bid him look on as he ran, and that he should give it in at the celestial gate: so they went their way. Then Christian gave three leaps for joy, and went on singing,

> "Thus far did I come laden with my sin,
> Nor could aught ease the grief that I was in,
> Till I came hither. What a place is this!
> Must here be the beginning of my bliss?
> Must here the burden fall from off my back?
> Must here the strings that bound it to me crack?
> Blest cross! blest sepulcher! blest rather be
> The Man that there was put to shame for me!"'

JOHN BUNYAN, *PILGRIM'S PROGRESS*

✠ SIGNIFICANT EVENTS IN THE 17th CENTURY

- The Protestant Reformation continues to affect the religious and political life of Europe.
- England begins to establish colonies in North America, many with the purpose of spreading Christianity — Jamestown begins in 1607, Pilgrims land in 1620, Massachusetts Bay Colony established by Puritans in 1630.
- In 1611 the *King James Version* translation of the English Bible published.
- In 1633 Galileo forced by the Inquisition to reject Copernicus' theories.
- In 1634 The first Oberammergau Passion Play.
- In 1649 In England — King Charles I beheaded.
- Classic works of Christian literature are written: Blaise Pascal's *Pensées*, 1670 ; John Bunyan's *Pilgrim's Progress*, 1678.

9.4 18TH TO 20TH CENTURIES

New ideas of the Enlightenment and discoveries in science, especially in geology and biology, seemed to attack many of the cherished beliefs of Christians. The 19th century, the great century of Christian mission, took the Christian faith to every corner of the known world. Despite the efforts of the members of the ecumenical movement in the 20th century, the divisions between the Protestants, Catholics, and Orthodox denominations remain wide.

William Wilberforce,
anti-slavery campaigner.

18th CENTURY

✚ MOST FAMOUS BIBLE CONCORDANCE

Alexander Cruden completed his concordance of the *King James Version* of the Bible in 1737. He wrote the following prayer in the preface to its first edition:

'I conclude this preface with praying that God, who has graciously enabled me to bring this large work to a conclusion, would make it useful to those who seriously and carefully search the Scriptures; and grant that the sacred writings, which are so important and worthy of high esteem, may meet with all that affection and regard which they deserve. May those who profess to believe the Scriptures to be a revelation

✚ SIGNIFICANT EVENTS IN THE 18th CENTURY

- An Evangelical awakening spreads throughout England and America under the preaching of George Whitefield, the Wesley brothers, and Jonathan Edwards.
- J.S. Bach's musical compositions.
- Count Zinzendorf and the Moravian Brethren begin their missionary work.
- Handel, Mendelssohn, and Haydn write Christian classical music.
- Isaac Watts and John Charles Wesley write hymns for congregational singing.
- Philip Doddridge writes *Rise and Progress of Religion in the Soul*. *Cruden's Bible Concordance* published.
- Religious freedom gains ground. In the United States, religious tests for government positions are abolished, and in Russia Czarina Catherine the Great grants freedom of religion.
- Era of modern missionary work. London *Baptist Missionary Society* commissioned William Carey to become a missionary in India.
- 1788 Wilberforce begins the movement which will result in the abolition of slavery.

from God, apply themselves to the reading and study of them; and may they, by the Holy Spirit of God, who inspired the Scriptures, be made wise for salvation through faith which is in Christ Jesus. Amen.'

ALEXANDER CRUDEN

19th CENTURY

✠ AMERICA'S LEADING 19th-CENTURY EVANGELIST

'One lesson I learned that night is that I must preach to press Christ upon the people then and there, and try to bring them to a decision on the spot. Ever since that night I have determined to make more of Christ than in the past.'

DWIGHT L. MOODY DESCRIBING THE FIRE WHICH, BY BURNING DOWN THE HALL WHERE HE HAD JUST ASKED PEOPLE TO THINK ABOUT CHRIST, PREVENTED THEM COMING BACK WITH THEIR DECISION.

- Protestants established missions throughout the world. *The British and Foreign Bible Society* (1804), the *American Bible Society* (1816), the *Sunday School Union*, and the *American Board of Commissioners of Foreign Missions* founded. *Salvation Army* founded in 1865.
- Charles Finney leads revival meetings.
- Dwight L. Moody and Ira Sankey hold large revival meetings on both sides of the Atlantic.
- Charles Spurgeon preaches in London's Metropolitan Tabernacle.
- David Livingstone opens up central Africa to missionary work through his mapping of the area. Hudson Taylor founds *China Inland Mission*.
- Pope Pius IX proclaims the Immaculate Conception of the Virgin Mary. In 1870 the First Vatican Council declares the pope infallible.

'There is no better evangelist in the wold than the Holy Spirit.'

DWIGHT L. MOODY

20th CENTURY

✠ ONE OF THE MOST INFLUENTIAL 20th-CENTURY THEOLOGIANS

'Jesus does not give recipes that show the way to God as other teachers of religion do. He is himself the way. The gospel falls upon man as God's own mighty Word, questioning him down to the bottom of his being, uprooting him from his securities and satisfactions, and therefore tearing clean asunder all the relations that keep him prisoner within his own ideals in order that he may be genuinely free for God and his wonderful new work of grace in Jesus Christ.

'In God alone there is faithfulness and faith in the trust that we may hold to him, to his promise and to his guidance. To hold to God is to rely on the fact that God is there for me, and to live in this certainty.'

KARL BARTH

✤ APOLOGY FOR THE CRUSADES

Members of 'The Reconciliation Walk' issued this press release in 1999:
'When have Christians demonstrated Christ's love to Muslims or Jews? We have gone to them with swords and guns. We have gone to them with racism and hatred. We have gone to them with feelings of cultural superiority and economic domination. We have gone to them with colonialism and exploitation. We have even gone to them with the gospel cloaked in arguments of superiority. Only a few have ever gone with the message of Calvary. We must do more than carry the message, we must be the message.'

✤ THE CRUSADES AND THEIR LEGACY OF HATRED

The mid-7th century to the mid-10th century saw the gradual expansion of Islam. Half of the Christian world was conquered by Arab armies. By the late 10th century, Europe and the Middle East were divided into Christian and Muslim spheres of influence. Christian pilgrims from Europe regularly visited Muslim-controlled Jerusalem in reasonable safety. Such pilgrimages were very popular. They were believed to be one of the major acts by which people could limit their exposure to the tortures of purgatory.

On November 27, 1095, Pope Urban II called on Europeans to go on a crusade to liberate Jerusalem from its Muslim rulers. The first and second wave of Crusaders murdered, raped and plundered their way up the Rhine and down the Danube as they headed for Jerusalem. The Crusaders demanded that the Jews either embrace the cross or die. 12,000 Jews in the Rhine Valley were killed as the first Crusade passed through, an event sometimes referred to as the 'first holocaust.' Once the Crusaders reached Jerusalem they discovered 6,000 Jews hiding in the synagogue. The Crusaders callously set the synagogue on fire, burning the Jews alive. Then

Christian mission uses modern advances to reach out to communities around the globe. An MAF plane and a Maasai group, Tanzania.

Many scientists today find that Christian belief and science relate.

30,000 Muslims who had fled to the al Aqsa Mosque were slaughtered without mercy.

These mass killings were repeated during each of the eight additional crusades until the final, ninth, crusade in 1272.

The press release of 'The Reconciliation Walk' stated: 'The Reconciliation Walk is an interdenominational grassroots movement of western Christians, retracing the route of the First Crusade, apologizing to Muslims, Jews and Eastern Christians for the atrocities of the Crusades: foremost among them, the misuse of the name and message of Jesus.'

500 participants reached Jerusalem on July 15, 1999, the 900th anniversary of the killing of about 60,000 Jerusalem residents and the destruction of the city.

About 2,000 Christians from 27 countries took part in this walk. Most were evangelical Protestants. Many wore T-shirts and caps with the slogan 'I apologize' in Arabic or Hebrew.

✠ CHRONOLOGY OF CHRISTIAN BROADCASTING

1921 (Jan 2): First religious broadcast aired by radio station KDKA.

1922 (Jun 17): First religious broadcast ministry launched by Paul Rader of Chicago.

1927 First woman radio operator is Lois Crawford of religious station KFGQ-AM/Boone IA.

1928 First network religious program launched by Donald Grey Barnhouse of Philadelphia.

1931 (Feb 22): First international religious station is Radio Vatican, beaming religious services across Europe.

1931 (Dec 25): First missionary radio station is HCJB, founded by Clarence Jones and Reuben Larson in Quito, Ecuador.

1940: First religious telecast is the Easter Sunday service of a local church that is telecast over W2XBS/New York.

1948 (Jan 1): First made-for-TV worship service produced, *The Lutheran Hour*, and aired on KSD-TV/St Louis.

1949: First evangelical on network TV is Percy Crawford with Youth on the March.

1957 (June 1): First television crusade with Billy Graham from New York is carried over the ABC network.

1961: First religious TV station, expressly licensed for religious programming, Pat Robertson's WYAH-TV/Portsmouth VA.

1966: First Christian talk show is hosted by Pat Robertson on WYAH-TV.

1971: First religious satellite broadcast made from the NRB convention in Washington DC to the Trans World Radio station at Bonaire.

1977 (Apr): First Christian satellite operator is Pat Robertson's Christian Broadcasting Network.

1977 (May 15): First 24-hour Christian station is KTBN-TV/Los Angeles, owned by Trinity Broadcasting Network.

1987 (Jan 4): Oral Roberts questioned about claim that God will 'take me home' unless supporters donate $8 million.

The Christian Book of Records
Hendrickson Publishers, Inc.
P.O. Box 3473
Peabody, Massachusetts 01961-3473

Copyright © 2002 John Hunt Publishing
Text copyright © 2002 Mark Water

ISBN 1-56563-633-3

Original edition published in English under
the title *Christian Book of Records* by John Hunt
Publishing Ltd, Alresford, Hants, UK.

Designed and produced by Tony Cantale Graphics

First printing – March 2002

Manufactured in Hong Kong/China